The Young Player's Guide to Cricket

The Young Player's Guide to Cricket

DEREK RANDALL
with **TERRY BOWLES**

David & Charles
Newton Abbot   London   North Pomfret (Vt)

British Library Cataloguing in Publication Data

Randall, Derek
  The young player's guide to cricket.
  1. Cricket
  I. Title   II. Bowles, Terry
  796.358   GV917
  ISBN 0-7153-7991-7

Typeset by Trade Linotype Limited, Birmingham
Printed in Great Britain
by Biddles Limited, Guildford, Surrey
for David & Charles (Publishers) Limited
Brunel House Newton Abbot Devon

Published in the United States of America
by David & Charles Inc
North Pomfret Vermont 05053 USA

Contents

Photography by Patrick Eagar

1

Review of World Cricket

Cricket lovers throughout the world will talk of Kerry Packer as a villain for years to come but I am not convinced that history books will reveal him in the same light. I have never had any links with the Australian television magnate and I am in no way attempting to defend the motives behind the formation of World Series Cricket. Yet I am becoming increasingly convinced that his interference was a good thing for cricket. That is not how it was designed, of course, and a few casualties have been claimed along the way, but unwittingly his breakaway group created a situation that, in the long term, can benefit the game immensely.

The instant reaction of the majority of people when Packer arrived on the scene in 1977 was to suggest it would lead to the end of cricket in its established form. That was perfectly understandable, and certainly the immediate consequences were bound to be severe.

Counties and countries lost their star players, the men who attract spectators and set the standards which others must attempt to match. Many deserted to 'the other side' and, in sporting terms, it was nothing less than war.

Yet as the dust begins to settle, it is now possible to recognise ways in which the advent of World Series Cricket helped to cement the future of the game. Just as the introduction of one-day cricket provided a desperately needed boost in the late 1960s, so Packer and his disciples forced the game into one of the most significant periods of its long history.

Inevitably, people had to pick sides and question their values in a way that few had done before. This was equally true of players and of authorities, and eventually led to an international closing of ranks as they fought with a common aim.

After two traumatic years, I sense that cricket in general has taken a leap forward in terms of preserving its status as a top professional sport.

It is not a situation that is likely to be repeated in the foreseeable future because the authorities will have learned a lot from their experiences. Yet the mere threat which Packer presented has encouraged people to adopt more modern thinking.

Cricket is a game with strong traditions. People enjoy clinging to the past and, in general, they do not take kindly to the idea of change. They continue to place emphasis on etiquette and given this, it is not surprising that they cringed at the prospect of Packer's teams taking the field in coloured outfits to play a floodlit match.

Yet, leaving the gimmicks aside, I feel that much can be learned from the World Series style of selling the game to the public. Commercially we have lagged behind and Packer's influence has helped to accelerate the trend towards catching up. It has also forced the authorities to recognise the value of top players and pay them accordingly. Leaving on one side the fact that I might be affected by this, it is, I think, a move that is absolutely essential to the future of international and domestic cricket.

Only time will tell whether my view of the Packer situation is accurate, but a close study of affairs in Australia over the next couple of years will provide us with a clearer guide. It will take at least that long for them to recover from the financial hardship caused by the World Series era, and as Australia undoubtedly suffered most, it is perhaps only fair that they should reap the greatest long-term benefits.

When England flew there for the 1978–9 tour, Australia had been placed in a position where they were forced to use players largely untried at international level. But although we won the series convincingly, I maintain that they did not let their country down. England coasted into a 2–0 lead. Yet they fought back well, and by the time we left for home, the Australians were vastly improved players.

Sunil Gavaskar is one of the most talented batsmen in the world. His ability is clearly illustrated by his outstanding Test record and India will rely heavily on him in the next few years while they undergo a rebuilding process

The benefits of that Test Match experience promised much for Australia's long-term prospects on the field and with the World Series players available again, strong competition for places was inevitable.

Able young cricketers like Kim Hughes, Allan Border and Rodney Hogg had emerged and with the return of formidable performers like Greg and Ian Chappell, Dennis Lillee and Rodney Marsh, Australia moved into the 1980s with much to look forward to.

The strength of their combined resources was perfectly illustrated when we returned on the hectic 1979–80 tour. England proved superior in the one-day matches but in the Tests, where it really mattered, we were outplayed.

Despite this, they showed they are not yet ready to challenge the supremacy of West Indies, who beat Australia on their own soil for the first time in a Test series.

Clive Lloyd's men were understandably labelled the kings of world cricket when they won the Prudential World Cup for the second time in succession in 1979. Such a title would need confirming in performances over five days but conclusive proof was duly provided in Australia.

The balance of power tends to change regularly in most sports – and thankfully so – yet West Indies seem to have been at the top now for many years, and although several of their finest players are drifting past their peak, such is their consistency that they will no doubt already have quality replacements lined up, awaiting their opportunity.

In Test Match terms, their bowling lacks variety. They have never been able to find a spinner to replace the great Lance Gibbs, but the sheer depth of talent they have available is almost frightening to think about. For example, who needs a spinner – even at international level – when you can pick from a pace attack of Michael Holding, Andy Roberts, Joel Garner, Wayne Daniel and Colin Croft? Line them up alongside four or five batsmen who are capable of taking on the opposition single-handed when the occasion demands and it does not take a genius to know why they are a successful combination.

Tony Greig was never allowed to forget his unfortunate comments a few years ago when he talked about making West Indies grovel when they are down. There might well have been some sound logic in what he said, but I am still waiting to see them in a position where his theory can be put to the test.

Because of their natural attacking instincts they have always tended to establish control at an early stage and once that happens, capturing the initiative from them can be impossible. I remember vividly the 1979 Prudential World Cup Final at Lord's when the England lads thought they had them struggling at two significant moments of the match. At lunch they were 90–4 and we felt that a couple more wickets would put us in a commanding position. Collis King soon put a stop to that line of thought with a superb innings and it took a tremendous effort on our part to keep us involved in the match. Then, when Geoff Boycott and Mike Brearley gave the

Joel Garner in action during the 1979 Gillette Cup Final at Lords. He contributed much to Somerset's season and, at 6ft 8in tall, is a formidable bowler to deal with

England innings an excellent base, we thought we detected signs that West Indies were beginning to panic. It was great for our confidence and we felt we had them, but big Joel Garner smashed through our middle-order batting and we were out of contention.

It is that type of individual flair that makes West Indies such dangerous opposition no matter what the circumstances, and no other country in the world can match them in this respect.

England have probably come closest to challenging West Indies in terms of international success in recent years, even though we let ourselves down badly on our trip to Australia.

Inevitably, people will say we were 'found out'. They will claim the England players were not of true international class and that this was highlighted once the World Series men returned to compete against us in Tests.

I offer no defence for our failures in Australia but although recognising that it is a matter of opinion, I would argue that the England lads deserve considerable credit for their run of success in the preceding years.

For reasons which I cannot understand, the English public always seem to be apologising for any success an international team gains, rather than simply enjoying it.

There is absolutely no way of knowing what might have happened had Pakistan and Australia been at full strength when we beat them – and if Tony Greig, Derek Underwood, Alan Knott and Bob Woolmer had been available for England. I would suggest, however, that we would have come out of those matches with a similar record simply because we had a very capable side.

The resurgence of the England team began under the captaincy of Greig when we went to India and won a series on their territory for the first time since World War II. The under-estimated Mike Brearley assumed control when Greig joined World Series and despite seemingly constant criticism, he carried on the good work in building a team which brought England success over a lengthy period. In Australia, for example, they had a weakened side, but

Glenn Turner is one of New Zealand's world-class performers. Their lack of depth makes it difficult to compete at international level but in the circumstances they do a fine job

such was the quality of our play on that tour that it would have taken a fine team to stop us winning the series.

England have come as close as any team to challenging the supremacy of West Indies in recent years, although I am always a bit surprised that Pakistan do not make a bigger impression in international cricket. Man for man, they can field a side almost as powerful as West Indies and they have the potential to become a great team.

It is essential to have outstanding players in key positions and Pakistan are well equipped in this respect. Imran and Sarfraz make up a formidable opening attack, and as you would expect on their 'flat' wickets, they have consistently produced magnificent stroke-makers like Majid Khan, Zaheer Abbas and Asif Iqbal. So why is it that they have never reached the heights you might expect from a team with players of this calibre in their ranks?

I can only imagine that they lack a strong leader, a man who is capable of sorting them out if the need arises; Pakistan would be a major force if they could add consistency to their game.

Without intending to be disrespectful, the difference in standard between the 'Big Four', and New Zealand and India, is at present quite wide.

It is always something of a struggle for New Zealand to compete at international level given that they do not have the same number of players to pick from as other cricketing nations. But in the circumstances, they do a marvellous job, as was underlined when they startled West Indies in 1980.

Their biggest problem is a lack of depth, and this is something they may never be able to overcome. They do currently have three world-class performers in Richard Hadlee, Glenn Turner and Geoff Howarth, and they rely heavily on these players.

India's predicament is a similar one at the moment, although their problems may be only temporary. In opener Sunil Gavaskar they have one of the finest batsmen in the world; his record speaks for itself. But apart from Viswanath and Vengsarkar, he is a long way above his colleagues in terms of class.

Although a totally different proposition in their own environment, India are in the process of rebuilding their team. Their top spinners, Chandrasekhar, Bedi and Prasanna, are moving towards

14

retirement and as key figures in the India team in recent years, they will not be replaced overnight.

The emergence of Kapil Dev and Ghavri has come with ideal timing because they are promising opening bowlers, capable of securing an early breakthrough and sharing the work-load with the spinners. In the past, India have tended to use their pace-men simply as a means of removing the shine from the new ball and then to rely on the spinners to bowl out the opposition.

This might not be possible any longer without those experienced spinners. But if the new quick-bowlers can establish themselves, it will allow India vital breathing space while their next generation of players is maturing.

Any review of world cricket would not be complete without devoting a section to South Africa, whose continued absence from the Test Match scene is a tragedy for lovers of good cricket and for the individuals good enough to play for that country.

Just sit down and write out a team of South Africans . . . Mike Procter, Graeme Pollock, Clive Rice, Ken McEwan, Garth Le Roux and so on. It is not hard to realise that they have something special to offer and would be formidable opponents if they were given the chance to join forces for a common cause.

They are victims of circumstances beyond their control, and I have tremendous sympathy with them as individuals. As professional sportsmen, and highly talented ones at that, they are denied the opportunity of performing at a level that is consistent with their ability.

I fully understand the reasons for banning South Africa from Test cricket, and perhaps this is one instance where politics should impinge on sport. But from a purely cricketing point of view, the sooner they are welcomed back into the fold the better it will be.

2

Structure of a County Cricket Club

Stroll into Trent Bridge any time you are passing and you will discover that Nottinghamshire County Cricket Club is run as an efficient business concern, geared towards making a healthy profit at the end of each financial year.

Although the committee still retains overall control and its members are responsible for general policy making, they came to terms some years ago with the fact that radical changes would have to be made. They decided the time had come to play a less prominent role themselves and to call in experts who would give the club a chance of surviving in the increasingly competitive world of professional sport.

Nottinghamshire now employ a chief executive, a general manager and an accountant – together with their respective staffs – whose job it is to deal with administration and ensure that sufficient money pours in to keep the club functioning.

At the same time, no one has lost sight of the fact that Nottinghamshire are in business to play cricket, and progressive changes have also been made in this sphere with the aim of producing a successful team. A cricket manager, Ken Taylor, was appointed in the closing weeks of the 1978 season and it is his responsibility to govern all aspects of the playing side.

It has been a remarkable transformation, especially when you consider the almost amateur way in which the game was run some years ago. In those days, the routine running of a county cricket club was the responsibility of the secretary who, more often than not, was tucked away in a corner somewhere. If fortunate, he had an assistant, but more commonly, his chief aide was a young lady who answered the telephone, opened the mail and typed a few letters.

For six months of the year, they were lonely people: the whole business revolved around playing cricket in the summer and the object of the exercise was to make enough money from Championship matches during the season to keep the club alive. Once the season had finished the club would virtually close down; and if attendances had been high enough throughout the summer months, a profit would be announced at the annual meeting.

By the mid-1960s, however, almost every county was in financial difficulty. Interest in three-day cricket had dropped off alarmingly and because of the unimaginative way in which most clubs operated, there were genuine fears about the game's chances of survival.

It needed something special to breathe fresh life into cricket, and the introduction of one-day competitions was a master-stroke at this time of crisis. Not only did the instant game re-awaken the interest of spectators: it also brought sponsorship into the sport on a scale never previously approached. Suddenly county cricket was becoming big business and it was no longer satisfactory to operate with an administrative staff of two or three, with committee members carrying out all other duties in a part-time capacity.

Committees have always been the power behind cricket clubs. Comprised of anything from a dozen to three dozen members, they meet regularly under the leadership of a chairman or president. Normally split into several sub-committees, they take responsibility for such items as finance, fund-raising and the upkeep of the ground, and their duties may entail about twenty hours of work a week. Under the old system, where everything revolved around the cash taken at the turnstiles, this was fine. Yet as the future of the game became increasingly more dependent on raising money through alternative means, so the need for more professional expertise became inevitable.

Nottinghamshire were the first club to appoint a chief executive to take the place of the old style secretary, and while Philip Carling continues to be in charge of day-to-day administration, he carries a much wider brief involving overall control of the staff and responsibility for increasing off-the-field income. Since his arrival the revenue at Trent Bridge has been boosted considerably, and clearly, when you are talking in terms of bringing in £350,000 a year as at some clubs, it takes a properly constituted and qualified staff to raise the money and handle it.

All clubs have been forced to adopt a more progressive outlook in the past few years, and to come to terms with the harsh fact that gate receipts alone will not keep them alive. In consequence, domestic cricket now functions on a far sounder basis.

Fortunately, the changes were made early enough for the game to survive in its traditional form. They were inevitable and they have spilled over into the playing side where clubs are at last coming to accept that full-time cricket managers are needed to relieve the burden on captains. I have always felt it was ludicrous that the man with responsibility for looking after his own game and directing operations on the field should also have administrative worries. Able captains are not necessarily able administrators but until recently, if you took on one job, you took on both.

Since the one-day competitions were introduced the pressures on captains have multiplied, and it is only right that they should have someone to lean on, someone who understands their problems and can advise them in times of trouble.

The manager has overall control of all cricket matters throughout the club – something the captain could only ever have in theory – and although he tends to do more administrative work than a football manager, he is answerable for results in just the same way. Since the advent of managers, far greater emphasis has been placed on scouting and coaching and it is hardly necessary to stress how important this is to the future of the game.

I was one of the fortunate youngsters in that I had the right connections to get me into the professional game. I did not play much cricket at school but I became involved with Retford, my local club, at an early age. Their captain Mike Hall had played for Nottinghamshire, and when I showed signs of potential with Retford in the Bassetlaw League, he made sure that those who mattered at Trent Bridge knew about this.

I was asked to join the ground staff after occasional 2nd XI appearances, and although I like to think I had enough talent to have broken through anyway, I sometimes wonder. Under the old system it was often the case that if you had not attended the right school or university, you were not given a second thought.

Nottinghamshire set a new trend in county cricket when they appointed Philip Carling as chief executive and their success has prompted other clubs to follow the example. As well as controlling the administration of the club, he also has overall charge of the staff and is responsible for off-the-field income

Scouting and coaching used to be a very disorganised business and I am convinced that many good youngsters have been missed because of this. The introduction of managers is already changing this unhappy trend, however, and because of their full-time involvement they are able to introduce schemes and to make sure they are followed through.

19

Considerably more attention is given to finding promising school-boys these days in that clubs are setting up scouting networks. Once discovered, they tend to be given coaching while still at the right age to benefit from it, and even if they cannot command a regular place in the county colts side, their progress in club cricket is monitored. In contrast to the situation when I started out in cricket, I would say that nowadays there is very little chance of a promising youngster missing out on an opportunity if he has the ability and inclination to make the grade.

The wind of change has certainly gusted through county cricket clubs in recent years. This is true to such an extent that perhaps the only area of staff structure which has not been altered concerns those who deal with the playing area. Maybe this is because in the case of ground staff, clubs have always employed the necessary expertise. Almost without exception, groundsmen do a magnificent job in often difficult circumstances and while this situation exists, why advocate change?

At Trent Bridge the head groundsman, Ron Allsopp, has two assistants and this department tends to be a law unto itself. Ron knows that questions will be asked if the pitches are not up to scratch but he is basically left to do things as he sees fit.

Of course, there is much more to his job than simply cutting the grass and sticking a few stumps into the ground. It takes twelve months a year to produce a carpet-like outfield and ideal cricket wickets which will bounce and seam at the start, flatten out to favour the batsmen, and then assist the spinners in the closing stages of a Championship game.

Good groundsmen are in short supply and they play a vital role in any cricket club. Constantly striving to beat the weather – and I do not just mean the rain – their life is often frustrating, and at times they work under severe pressure.

At grounds where television cameras are frequently in use, they must make sure that on such occasions the pitch is ideally positioned and that advertising boards are not obscured by the sight-screens. These may sound like incidental little items, but it is typical of the things which the groundsman must consider when he maps out his match by match pitch rota at the start of the season.

3

Batting

So often you find that things happen in life which at the time carry little significance; yet when you look back on them years later, it is possible to discover that they had a major effect on your future.

There is no better example of this where I am concerned than the stick and the tennis ball – my two favourite toys. I could not count the hours I spent throwing the ball against a wall at home and getting into position to meet it when it rebounded.

That old stick was little more than two inches thick and I wish I still had it because that, more than anything, pointed me in the right direction. There is no finer form of practice for a hopeful young batsman because it forces you to do all the essentials. If I was not perfectly positioned, concentrating on keeping my head over the ball and watching it all the way onto the end of the stick, there was no chance of me making contact. It was an uncomplicated exercise but after spending countless hours working at it, playing with a cricket bat was relatively easy in comparison.

In those days, I used to imagine I was Tom Graveney. He was my great idol because he struck the ball so firmly yet so effortlessly. His timing was superb and no matter who was bowling to him, he seemed to be in position waiting for the ball to arrive. It was inevitable, I suppose, that I would try to copy Graveney's mannerisms as closely as possible, in the same way as I regularly see young lads in Nottinghamshire adopting the Tony Greig style of stance which our captain Clive Rice uses.

I realise that trying to stop a youngster from impersonating his hero would be an impossible mission despite the fact that in the long run, such impersonation can do more harm than good. Batting is a natural thing, and it is very important to develop your own style and bat in the way which suits you best.

To give an example of the harm which can be done by trying to copy someone, it is only a few years since I decided I must study the methods employed by Geoff Boycott. I had been having a difficult time and in trying to analyse my faults I decided to go back to basics, pick on the most correct player around, and attempt to emulate him.

When it comes to technique, there is none better than Boycott. His immaculate defence ensures he seldom fails when he goes to the wicket, and his dedication and powers of concentration make him the consistently fine player he is. Geoff is a touch player who sets out to wear the bowlers down. He is superb at finding the gaps and is content to work the ball around and make the bulk of his runs in singles rather than boundaries.

My confidence had deserted me and the runs had stopped flowing when I went to Pakistan with England. In the circumstances, attempting to adopt the Boycott style seemed a logical thing to do.

My problems quickly multiplied, however, and when I look back on that difficult time, I realise how stupid I was in thinking myself capable of going from one extreme to another. I have a tremendous admiration for Boycott and often wish I had some of his attributes. But my style is to go out and attack the ball. That experience in Pakistan taught me that even when you stop making runs – as inevitably you must at some stage – to suddenly change your whole approach to batting is not something which can be undertaken lightly.

I found myself in a similar predicament on the latest tour of Australia when, after a very satisfying start, I totally lost my touch. The runs suddenly dried up and after a succession of failures, I eventually lost my England place.

Obviously, I would have done anything humanly possible to solve the problems but deep down, I knew that the only solution was to do it my way – the way which had earned me England selection in the first place.

Geoff Boycott shows his style in the 1979 Test against India at the Oval. He is the most correct batsman around and his immaculate defence, dedication to his job and remarkable powers of concentration make him the consistently fine player he is

Obviously there are things which can – and will – be learned from studying the great players. Apart from all else, the top men set standards which others have to try and match – that is what competitive sport is all about. Players do not become great by studying the textbooks or other individuals, however. They make it to the top by expressing their ability in a way which comes naturally and they all have their own trademark – something which detaches them from the rest and makes them special.

In the case of Gary Sobers it is difficult to pinpoint one facet because he had everything. He was the best batsman I have ever seen, and I will always be proud of the fact that I began my professional career under his captaincy at Trent Bridge.

Sobers was a cricketing genius. There were times when you felt he could do things at will and when he was in the mood, he would strike the ball with frightening power. There was surely never a more fluent player, and although only a couple of thousand people had the privilege of seeing the innings, I doubt if he ever showed his greatness to better effect than in a Championship game against Derbyshire. It was a slow pitch on which everyone was struggling to get the ball away yet in strolled Sobers to make the fastest 100 of the season which left us gasping with envy.

That was Gary at his best, and I suppose the nearest to him in modern cricket is his fellow West Indian, Viv Richards. There is a touch of greatness about the way he gets into position early and cracks respectable deliveries away with such power that the fielder does not stand a chance. Although happiest when he can play in typical cavalier style, he showed with his century in the 1979 Gillette Cup Final that he can get his head down and bat responsibly when the situation demands.

I have already discussed the virtues of Boycott, the master technician. Leicestershire's David Gower is another player for whom I have a tremendous respect. He is a stylish batsman whose great strength is in his timing, and perhaps it is because he has the same

A typically fluent stroke earns more runs for David Gower. Timing is the great strength of the stylish Leicestershire and England batsman and his natural ability makes him the envy of cricketers throughout the world

apparently effortless approach as Tom Graveney that I admire him so much.

All the batsmen I have mentioned have their own individual styles, and although I am not knocking the coaching manuals – it is right for youngsters to know the textbook way of doing things – I am a firm believer in each player doing what is right for him.

Whenever I step out to bat, I go through the same little ritual. I glance around the sky to help my eyes get accustomed to the light and then take a concentrated look at the sight-screen because this is the background which, hopefully, I will be working with for the next few hours.

Next on my list of priorities as I approach the wicket is to study the pitch. This is where the ball will bounce and move when it comes flying towards me – possibly at ninety miles per hour – within the next couple of minutes and it is no good complaining that I could not pick it up as my middle stump is uprooted.

Taking guard is often regarded as a pointless formality by many youngsters but do not underestimate its value. One of the most important things about batting is to know exactly where your stumps are at all times because you need to recognise instinctively which ball is likely to hit them.

My own preference for guard is middle-and-leg and I stick to this except, possibly, when I am batting on a turning wicket against a left-arm spinner. In this instance, I normally switch to middle-and-off and am looking to be positioned on the off side of the ball at all times.

The next thing to consider is where the fielders are positioned and a useful tip is to try to memorise who is standing where. Experience teaches you to respect certain fielders and provided you are concentrating properly, this will minimise the chances of a run out. If I am playing for Nottinghamshire against Middlesex, for example, I will take special note of the fact that Graham Barlow is stationed in the covers, and I will know not to risk any quick singles if the ball is played to the left hand of Phil Edmonds.

It is not simply a matter of knowing where the main danger men are, however, because any of the fielders is capable of getting you out and you must be alert to this possibility. Once you have been in for two or three overs, if someone said 'cut' and froze the action you should be able to draw a diagram indicating where every single fielder is placed.

I was guilty of losing concentration in a Championship match against Middlesex in 1979. I was already in the eighties, moving along nicely, and Phil Edmonds had taken John Emburey away from leg slip and sent him to extra cover. A couple of overs later though, Emburey drifted back to leg slip and I did not pick him up. Consequently, when I turned a ball from Edmonds round the corner and set off for a single he very nearly caught me out of my ground. In the end, I went on to make a double-century but that lapse in concentration could have denied me the best score of my career.

Concentration is of primary importance at all times when you are at the crease and initially, this needs to be coupled with patience. A good innings is built on a solid foundation and unless circumstances demand it, there is little point in arriving at the crease intent on smashing the ball around the ground from the start.

The best policy is to aim at allowing as many balls as possible to pass harmlessly by in the early overs, and this is why your guard is so important: it ensures you are always aware of where the stumps are. Restricting yourself to not playing across the line or wild shots outside off stump naturally cuts down your chances of an early dismissal, and there are other advantages in employing these tactics. Every delivery which passes by untouched tires and disheartens the bowlers. At the same time, the ball is becoming more worn, and you are getting more accustomed to the pace of the wicket and the conditions.

The experts say that in the initial stages of an innings it is best to play in a 'V' between mid-on and mid-off and this is sound advice. Those who stick to this principle in the first half hour will not go far wrong. By this time, you might have twenty or so runs to your name and you will be growing in confidence and ready to attempt the more adventurous shots.

No matter which facet of batting is under discussion, the need for a high level of concentration is prominent on any list of priorities. Relax at your peril – and this applies just as much when you are standing at the non-striker's end.

I had this lesson forced home to me in the harshest possible way when batting with Geoff Boycott during an England tour of Pakistan. It was an incident I am never likely to forget. Boycott is good at clipping the ball off his legs for a single behind square and because they had a man on the fence, he had already scored a few in this way. The opposing captain soon got wise to his favourite trick, however, and when he moved the fielder in ten yards I was not concentrating hard enough to notice it. This was to prove fatal because when I called Geoff for a run the next time he played that stroke, then had to send him back, it caused him to be run out.

The principle in calling is for the non-striker to decide whether a run is possible when the ball goes behind the stumps, while the striker covers anything in front of the stumps. It is a simple policy which is normally successful although the trend has changed since the introduction of the one-day game.

Batting in limited-overs cricket is to some extent a different art, with much greater emphasis being placed on scampering quick singles. Being able to judge whether a run is possible can make the difference between winning and losing, and if you want to avoid disaster, it is essential to know how long it takes your partner to run 22 yards. If it takes him two seconds longer than you to cover that distance then it is vital you know this and do not put his wicket at risk.

We have now adopted a system at Trent Bridge whereby both batsmen call at the same time with each saying whether a run is possible for him. The rule is that if either says no, you stay where you are.

It is easy enough to set down hard and fast rules on batting but as I have already stressed, it is very necessary to retain an individual style and a degree of versatility. For example, different circumstances and playing conditions will demand that a batsman adapts, and if he cannot, he will not survive.

My ideal batting conditions are a hot, sunny day and a pitch with some bounce and pace in it. I am not particularly strong, and in these conditions, I find it is easier to force the ball away. Being basically a back foot player who scores many of his runs by cutting and pulling, that bit of extra bounce and pace enables me to stand up and play my shots.

There are many batsmen who prefer slower, more predictable pitches where they can grind the bowlers down. But whatever our personal preferences, we must learn to cope with all types of conditions.

When conditions are perfect for batting, the best advice I can give is to make the most of things and enjoy yourself, for there will be plenty of occasions when the bowlers are dominant. Settle in patiently and then go on to express yourself in your own way.

If the ball is swinging or seaming the idea is to get forward onto the front foot where possible and play as late as you can. But on a turning wicket the technique required is totally different. The basic principle in these conditions is to be positioned towards the off stump so that you are over that side, waiting for the ball to arrive.

The batsman's nightmare, of course, is a wet or drying wicket, and if you are confronted by someone like Derek Underwood in such circumstances, there is no known counter for the bowling.

Either you should get down the wicket in an attempt to smother the ball or you should go in with the intention of striking every delivery as hard as you can and collect as many runs as possible while your luck holds. Either way, there is an element of risk involved, but there are no other alternatives as far as I am concerned.

Coping with the varying conditions is one of the most demanding aspects of batting and because I consider that youngsters should learn to bat in good conditions, I am delighted to hear that many schools are taking advantage of the new synthetic pitches which are now available.

When I was a lad in the process of learning the game it was seldom that I got the opportunity to practise on a good surface. This new innovation is doing the game a great service, and I am convinced that as synthetic pitches become more widely used, so we will develop more natural stroke-players in this country.

These pitches are ideal for practising batting techniques because of their consistency. The true bounce of the ball enables you to judge your shots more correctly and eliminates the fear of being struck on the head by a rising delivery – something which has often driven youngsters away from cricket in the past.

I cannot see the day arriving when synthetic pitches will be used for first-class matches: they are too predictable and give the batsmen an unfair advantage. However, they are perfect for teaching, and once a young player has mastered the basic principles of batting in conditions which are ideal for him, he will be better equipped to cope with the demands of a wet or turning wicket.

Defensive Strokes

These are the most important of all strokes because, quite simply, if you cannot defend your stumps then your chances of occupying the crease long enough to make a big score are negligible. The objective is to play a 'dead' bat shot which will block the ball and keep you out of difficulty. Depending on where the ball pitches, this is achieved with either a forward or backward stroke.

To play forward requires going onto the front foot with the bat and pad close together. The head must be very still and in line with the delivery, with the elbow high to ensure the ball is played into the ground.

Backward defensive is a natural alternative when the ball bounces or is pitched short. In this instance the batsman should be on the back foot, as upright and well-balanced as possible, and with the bat angled downwards.

On English wickets, where the ball generally comes through low, the tendency is to make a forward movement instinctively. On the more bouncy wickets of Australia, however, the backward defensive stroke is an essential part of the batsman's survival kit.

Driving Strokes

These are a slight variation on defensive strokes except that you finish with a follow-through. The positioning of the feet and body is much the same but, rather than blocking the ball, the intention is to force it away with as much power as possible.

The cover-drive is regarded by many as the classic stroke and there is no doubt that a sweetly-timed boundary through this area gives immense satisfaction to batsmen.

My favourite shot is the drive through mid-wicket and an analysis of my run-scoring over the years would doubtless reveal that a high percentage have come from hits in this region.

The Pull and the Hook

These are similar attacking shots which more often than not will lead to leg-side boundaries if efficiently executed.

The pull is used to deal with a delivery which is short of a good length, and it involves moving the body into a position in line with the ball and rolling the wrists to keep it down.

If the ball is especially short, so that it needs to be played at virtually head height, then the hook can be employed. It is similar to the pull but because of the difficulty in controlling this shot, many players opt to duck under the ball in preference to taking the risk.

I find the hook is a good percentage shot for me and I normally go for it. I have sometimes lost my wicket because of this, but it has also earned me a lot of runs.

I will admit, however, that I have been guilty in the past of going for the hook too early in my innings, before becoming properly accustomed to the light and conditions. It is most definitely a shot to avoid until you are properly settled in because if bowlers know you can be tempted, they will keep you busy with a regular supply of short deliveries.

The Cut

Whether it be the square or late cut, these are other strokes which it is best to avoid until you are comfortably settled and seeing the ball well. The priorities are good positioning – inside the line of the ball with the foot well across – and ensuring that the wrists are rolled at the point of contact so that the ball is played into the ground.

Derek Randall illustrates the sweep in three stages. Notice how he moves to the pitch of the ball with head over it, plays it instinctively into the ground and fluently follows through while maintaining perfect balance throughout the stroke. It is the ideal counter against a spin bowler when the ball is turning towards the leg-side

The Sweep

This is perhaps the least effectively played and most misunderstood of batting strokes in lower grades of cricket, and yet it is vital for handling the spinners on a turning wicket.

As a youngster, I was told it was a shot which should never be played. This information was totally wrong and it took me a long time to sort things out and to accept that there was a place for the sweep in the right conditions.

I agree that it is a risky shot on a good wicket, but when the ball is turning and the bowler is pitching it on the off stump and making it spin abruptly to leg, the sweep is an effective shot to play.

In fact, I would suggest it should be employed from the start of an innings when conditions are favouring the spinners. The only real danger is from the straight delivery, and it is up to the batsman to 'pick' these and avoid being trapped leg-before-wicket.

4

Bowling

If I woke up one morning to discover I had mastered the art of fast-bowling, I would be delighted. It would only be a temporary feeling, however, because once I had delivered a few bouncers to certain individuals who have made life uncomfortable for me in the past, the sooner I was recognised as a batsman again, the better I would like it.

Fast-bowling is not a job which appeals to me. In some respects it is the most glamorous role in the profession, but I reckon that fast-bowlers are entitled to all the success they achieve. The life span of a top fast-bowler is comparatively short in the cricketing sense, and this is hardly surprising when you consider what they put into a week's work.

A 30-yard sprint can be exacting at the best of times, and when you have to do it six times straight off, then start again five minutes later, it can be a wearing business. The strain it puts on the muscles, especially the back, is incredible and it is rare indeed for a genuinely quick bowler to go through a complete season without a troublesome injury.

Top-class fast-bowlers make the difference between a team being successful or not. They are the match-winners and have to be nursed along so that they can function at maximum efficiency for as much of the season as possible. The demands placed on them in modern cricket are exacting and counties have come to recognise that they must be used in short, sharp bursts.

The 'quickies' are at their most dangerous when they have the new-ball to work with. It is a potentially lethal weapon in cricket terms and the amount of success they have in an opening spell almost invariably dictates the pattern of a match. Not only is the bowler fresh and at his most aggressive, he has everything working

34

in his favour at the outset. The shine on the new-ball will help it to swing – a tremendous amount if conditions are helpful – but the biggest advantage is the extra bounce he will get. This can vary from two inches to a foot, and a hostile opening burst can make life extremely uncomfortable for the batsmen.

By the time the opening bowlers come back for their second spell, the ball will be older and the pitch gradually losing its pace. It will then be much more difficult to make the breakthrough so it is vital that they take advantage of conditions while they are in their favour.

Inevitably the fielding side are on the attack when the ball is new and it is not unusual to see three slips, two gulleys, a leg slip and a forward short leg in these circumstances. With only a cover-point and mid-on in run-saving positions, the bowler is quite likely to be hit for a few boundaries, but he must not allow this to deter him.

His job is to force the batsman into errors by whatever means are possible, because if he does not provide an early breakthrough, it could mean his team will struggle for the remainder of the match.

Control is not always easy when you are running in at full speed, concentrating every ounce of energy on pace, but somehow this must be achieved because it is pointless having a ring of slip fielders if you are sending the ball down the leg-side. The ideal line for an orthodox fast-bowler is on or just outside off-stump. If the ball then moves away it is likely that the slip fielders will be in business, and if it nips back, you have a chance of trapping the batsman leg before wicket.

Dennis Lillee is a master at landing the ball in the danger area, and because of this consistency, you are constantly aware that you could be out to every ball he releases. Lillee gets the movement while his Australian partner Jeff Thomson is equally menacing for different reasons. He tends to pitch it short of a length and consequently you are playing the majority of his deliveries around chest height. When fully fit, Thomson is the quickest around and because of the extra bounce he gets, he can be a real handful.

Joel Garner is another bowler who gets plenty of bounce, but whereas Thomson finds it through sheer pace, Garner's asset is his exceptional height. Actually, they are both difficult customers to bat against – more so than orthodox fast bowlers.

I have played against Garner when his hand has disappeared above the top of the sight-screen at the moment he released the ball and believe me, it is not easy to play one of his deliveries when you cannot see the ball until it is virtually on top of you. In contrast, Thomson tends to hide it behind his back until the last possible moment and then sling it at you with his javelin thrower's action. At his pace this can cause severe problems, and although Lillee, and Michael Holding – who is the quickest of the West Indians – are guaranteed to trouble a batsman with their speed and control, at least you can follow the ball the whole way.

It is interesting making the comparison between some of the finest quick bowlers in the world today. Andy Roberts comes into this category, although he differs from the others in relying less on pace and more on thought. He realised some time ago that there is little point in charging in and sending down the ball as fast as he can. When he lets one go he is as quick as anyone, but these days he

Australia's Jeff Thomson is the quickest bowler around when fully fit and his ability to get extra bounce makes him a difficult man to handle. An added problem in facing Thomson is that he 'hides' the ball behind his back until the last moment

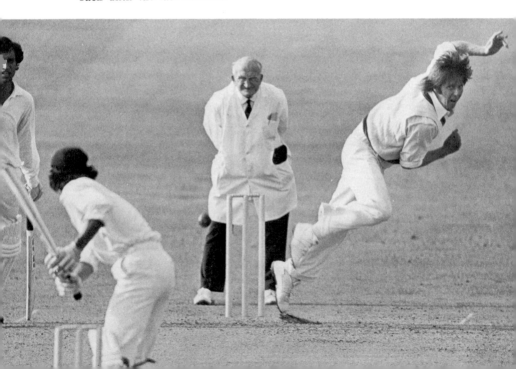

prefers to vary his pace. It is as though he is playing his own little game with the batsman and I must admit, guessing what he might do next certainly keeps you on your toes.

The five bowlers I have mentioned have let a few bouncers go in their time, and the short-pitched delivery is an essential part of their armoury. It is their surprise ball which, properly delivered, always has a chance of earning them a wicket. Those batsmen who do not get an edge with a self-defensive stroke are quite likely to do so attempting a hook.

Batsmen accept this as part of the game and I think fast-bowlers in England got a rough deal when a law was introduced in 1979 limiting them to one bouncer per over in Championship matches. Using the bouncer as a means of intimidation is wrong, of course, but I feel it should be left to the umpires to decide whether this is the case rather than telling the bowlers they can use one and one only. Perhaps I am biased because I enjoy playing the hook stroke but it certainly would not bother me if, within reason, bowlers were allowed to use a few more short balls.

In fact, being a fast-bowler in England – I mean genuinely fast – can be a thankless job and I do not think it is any coincidence that we have not produced very many in recent years. Fast, bouncy pitches are ideal for them and although virtually every groundsman in the country strives to produce these, relatively few succeed. Because of this, many promising youngsters are forced to cut down their pace and to concentrate more on line and length.

To take this a stage further, Sussex's Tony Pigott probably has a better chance of developing than have any of the younger brigade because he can do half a season's work on the consistently quick wickets at Hove. In contrast, although Graham Dilley, who toured Australia with England in 1979–80, has the potential to become the best quick bowler in the country it is debatable whether he will be able to fulfil this. He will probably be good enough to play for his country for many years, but I will be surprised if he develops into a bowler of genuine pace.

Dilley will play most of his cricket on the generally slow Kent wickets – especially Canterbury – and like his colleague Kevin Jarvis, may have to accept the situation and eventually cut his pace. Jarvis found it was pointless pounding in and attempting to bounce the ball on a pitch which would not respond and although he is still a fine bowler, it is disappointing from an English viewpoint that his potential as a genuine quickie is unlikely to be fulfilled.

England's shortage of really quick bowlers is not a problem in the international sense, however, because we have more top-quality fast-medium men than any country in the world.

There are two types of medium pacer – the seamers and those who swing the ball – and from a personal point of view I am less comfortable against this type of bowling than against someone who is formidably quick.

There is no better seamer playing cricket than Derbyshire's Mike Hendrick, and on a 'green' wicket he can be devastating. You can virtually guarantee that whether the ball be old or new, Hendrick will land every delivery on the seam and persuade it to deviate. He is a formidable opponent. If weather conditions are favouring

Whether the ball is old or new, Mike Hendrick lands virtually every delivery on the seam and makes the ball deviate. There is no better seam bowler playing cricket today and on a green pitch he can be devastating

the swing bowlers, the likes of Ian Botham and John Lever are every bit as difficult to deal with. Botham has had amazing success in his comparatively short time on the international scene and it speaks volumes for the depth of English bowling that Lever has been unable to command a regular Test place in recent years.

Lever is a left-armer, of course, and left-armers normally find it easier to keep the batsman tied down. Their most common delivery is angled across the right-handed batsman towards the slips but their most effective ball is the one which swings back and is always likely to earn a leg-before-wicket decision. In general terms, left-armers find it more difficult to take wickets and bearing this in mind, what Lever achieved for Essex in 1979 was nothing short of phenomenal.

I have always felt that left-armers are penalised by the law which allows only two men behind square on the leg side. There was a time when they could bowl big in-swingers and expect to get wickets from them. However, they are now a total waste of time, because with only a leg-slip and fine-leg covering a large area it is comparatively simple for the batsman to find the gaps.

Control is essential for the medium-pace bowlers. They can get more movement than the really fast men and it is important that they take full advantage of this. When conditions suit they must be sure to get among the wickets for there will be plenty of occasions when they will be asked to bowl for long periods with little hope of achieving anything other than keeping the batsmen quiet.

Although it is generally easier to remain at the crease when facing the lesser-paced bowlers, scoring runs against them is often a difficult business. They tend to operate with more defensive fields and more often than not, will pick up wickets by frustrating the batsmen. This is why bowling a consistently good line and length is so vital. If a batsman is not making runs he must alter his tactics to do something about it and it is then that he becomes vulnerable. When conditions are not helping the medium pacers they must rely on the batsmen making mistakes and if they persevere for long enough, they often get their reward.

Drying or dusty conditions are ideal for the spinners though slightly quicker bowlers sending down cutters can sometimes be even more unplayable. Paddy Clift of Leicestershire is especially effective at this and it surprises me that more bowlers of his pace do not achieve the same success.

When it comes to wet wickets, of course, one bowler stands out. Derek Underwood is in a class of his own and I doubt if anyone will ever produce an effective formula for countering him in these conditions. But it is not only on wet wickets that Underwood shines, for in my opinion he rates just ahead of Bishen Bedi as the best left-arm spinner in the world today. Their styles are contrasting but when it comes to effect, both can cause batsmen huge problems.

Underwood is far quicker than the majority of spinners and he makes the ball bounce more than most. His greatest asset is his immaculate control and even when the pitch is not assisting him, he will still do a tremendous job for his team because of his uncanny accuracy. I doubt whether there is a spin-bowler in cricket today who is more difficult to hit.

While Underwood spins the ball viciously with two fingers, Bedi adopts a totally different style. He flicks it through all his fingers – rather like spinning a top – and unless I am on the receiving end, I find him a delight to watch. The Indian master is a very casual bowler and he relies on guile and flight. Bedi spins the ball a tremendous amount and because of this, he gets turn on a pitch where no other bowler would manage it. When you watch from the pavilion the ball appears to be floating from one end to the other. But trying to judge the length of each delivery when you are facing him can sometimes be impossible.

To the right-handed batsman, the most common delivery from an orthodox left-arm spinner turns from leg to off whereas the off-spinner will move the ball from off to leg. Players like myself with a natural preference for hitting towards the leg side are reasonably comfortable against off-spinners, but this type of bowler causes problems for those who play predominantly towards the off-side.

Most English counties have at least one useful off-spinner in

On a wet wicket Derek Underwood is unplayable and even when conditions are not favouring him, the Kent left-arm spinner is an outstanding bowler. His immaculate control makes him one of the most difficult spin-bowlers to hit – a valuable asset in limited-overs matches

their ranks so that with the likes of John Emburey, Geoff Miller and Peter Willey to choose from, England are in this respect well equipped for Test matches. Miller relies mainly on swing and turn and, like Fred Titmus, can produce an effective floating delivery. I always find Emburey the most demanding to deal with, however, because he gets plenty of bounce and is a difficult bowler to sweep.

The golden rule against all forms of slow bowling is to hit with the spin. I have most problems against leg-spinners, and although from a batsman's point of view I am not sorry that they are a disappearing breed, this is a tragedy for cricket in general.

Leg-spin is a very attacking form of bowling and the exponents of this difficult art have suffered more than anyone from the move towards more defensive methods in cricket. Tactics have changed considerably since the introduction of the one-day competitions and the decision to restrict the first innings to one hundred overs in Championship matches. Run-saving is all-important these days. Dismissing a batsman can become less of a priority than stopping him scoring and, as a result, leg-spinners have been squeezed out of the first-class game.

Only Intikhab and Robin Hobbs have survived. Both are at the veteran stage and when they move into retirement it could mean the sad end of an era.

The problem with leg-spinners is that they seldom have the same control as the orthodox finger-spinners and, although they regularly get wickets, they give away runs in the process. They can only attack and while their best deliveries are often unplayable, they cannot be relied upon to keep down the scoring rate.

Their main deliveries are the leg-break and googly, and most can also bowl the top spinner which goes straight on after pitching, often keeping low. Perhaps it is because we so seldom come up against this form of bowling that we find it so hard to deal with,

Ian Botham has had amazing success with both bat and ball in his comparatively short time on the international scene. One of the most attacking bowlers around, he is a regular match-winner if conditions help him to swing the ball

and sometimes I find difficulty in picking out the leg break from the googly.

You do not see many young bowlers developing the art of leg-spin bowling these days but as I have said, it will be a tragedy if it disappears from the game completely.

There are several forms of practice for bowlers but in view of the importance of keeping a good line and length – no matter which style is used – I do not think you can better an exercise I once saw Fred Titmus working on.

Nottinghamshire were playing against Middlesex and I had just been dismissed early in the day when I saw Fred making his way to the nets. He was recovering from injury at the time and was anxious to get back into his normal consistent rhythm. I watched him place a square of paper on a good length and for the next two hours, he worked non-stop at trying to land the ball on it.

Regardless of your pace or variety of bowling, try seeing how many times out of six you can hit a piece of paper. If you manage it more times than you miss, you can say you have good control.

5

Fielding

My career as a professional cricketer was officially launched the day I collected a catch off the bowling of Gary Sobers. He was captain of Nottinghamshire at the time and although I had been on the Trent Bridge staff a few months and scored some runs, I had got the impression that no one had noticed me.

My involvement with the first-team players had been negligible until the day I was named as twelfth man for a Championship game against Hampshire and was called upon to field as substitute.

I was immediately sent down to fine leg and when a delivery from Sobers was sent soaring in my direction by Danny Livingstone, I managed to cling on to one of the best catches of my career. Sobers was delighted – as any bowler would have been – and although hardly anyone knew my name at the start of play, it was not too long before I was being offered a first-team opportunity.

There is no doubt in my mind that my fielding got me into the Nottinghamshire team initially and the same is true of every other level of cricket at which I have played.

My first contact with the England team was as twelfth man for a Test at Trent Bridge against New Zealand when, by tradition, they pick on a local player who is likely to save a few runs if his services are required. I am equally sure my fielding was taken into consideration when I got my first England cap. It stands to reason that if you have a couple of young batsmen of about the same ability and one is a better fielder, he will get the vote.

To develop this a stage further, there was a time in 1979 when my England place seemed in jeopardy because I was not making runs with consistency. But I hung on, thanks to those who pointed out the number of runs I managed to save in a day.

Throughout my career, my ability in the field has given me

opportunities which might not otherwise have been possible and I am just thankful, partly for my good luck and partly because I managed to recognise the importance of fielding at an early stage.

As a youngster with my home-town Club of Retford I was lucky if I got fifteen minutes of batting practice in the nets but after that, I could either go home or spend the next two hours fielding. Every night I was out there after school chasing the ball about, often until we literally needed the moon to help us see. When I think back though, those sessions were the making of me because although I like to think I am a better than average fielder, it did not all come naturally.

Enthusiasm and hard work were the vital ingredients at that stage, plus the realisation that if I was going to make the grade I would have to do more than simply score a few runs. In modern

Derek Randall brilliantly runs out Gordon Greenidge to give England a superb start against West Indies in the 1979 Prudential World Cup Final. His throw at the stumps scored a direct hit to leave Greenidge stranded – the result of hours of practice

cricket, you have to be exceptional to survive at the top as a specialist in just one aspect of the game.

Most batsmen can bowl a bit or vice versa, but as I could never get the hang of bowling properly, it left me with only one alternative.

Going back to my Retford days in the Bassetlaw League: I realised that I would not get into the team in any of the key batting positions, and numbers six, seven and eight in the order were normally reserved for the all-rounders or for bowlers who were useful batsmen. I had to force my way into the team some other way and when I finally made it, my fielding kept me in. I often went a few games without getting the chance to bat but by maintaining reasonable standards in the field, I was regarded as worth my place.

I am fortunate because I am reasonably quick and agile, and have big hands and gangly arms. Perhaps these attributes give me an advantage over most people but if you ask for my secret, I can only tell you that my reputation was earned by hard work.

Fielding – and fielding practice – is often regarded as the boring part of cricket. This is especially true at schoolboy level where it is seen as a means of filling in the time before a youngster gets his chance to bat or bowl. I can understand this, remembering only too well how difficult it was at times to work at improving my fielding when I might have been concentrating on the more glamorous aspects of the game.

It was not always easy, for example, disciplining myself to turn up at Trent Bridge in the middle of winter, stick one stump in the ground and spend the next couple of hours collecting a ball and trying to knock it over. That is what I mean about hard work but, I can assure you, it is worth doing in the long run.

I eventually reached a stage where I got as much pleasure from fielding as from batting and if I arrive for a Championship match and discover we have lost the toss, the prospect of a hard day in the field does not bother me.

It is absolutely vital to approach the job with enthusiasm. There are not a lot of rewards to be had and you have to go out and make your own satisfaction. I find that the best way to do this is by setting myself a target and starting the day intent on keeping a clean sheet. My aim is not to concede a single run, and if I can leave the field knowing no batsman pinched a single because I was dreaming, or a boundary which sneaked through my hands, then I know I have helped to serve my team.

Consistently good fielding – especially close catching – wins matches, and when I picked up a Benson and Hedges' Gold Award for my work in the field in a game against Northamptonshire, it caused quite a stir in the Nottinghamshire dressing room. Some of the lads felt this was out of order but I defended the decision. Although I was the fortunate one who got the award, our fielding undoubtedly earned us the points in that match.

Bowlers respond to sharp, enthusiastic fielding. They become keyed up if they know their colleagues are on their toes, anxious to prevent any runs being scored, and once the batsman is forced to take chances because the bowling and fielding is so tight, the initiative has been gained.

In the better grades of cricket, bowlers tend to bowl to their field. They place their most reliable fielders in key positions – at mid-wicket for an off-spinner for example – and attempt to bowl in such a fashion that the batsman can only hit the ball to that area.

People often assume that I must have modelled myself on a particular fielder but this is not really the case. Obviously there have been several players I admired, but as with batting, I do not think anyone can get to the top by copying another person's style.

There are a tremendous number of splendid fielders in the game today, but there have been none better in my opinion than Clive Lloyd. For such a big chap he was a magnificent mover and covered such a vast area that it was always difficult to judge whether or not a run was possible when the ball was hit in his direction.

Perhaps the man who made the biggest impression on me as a youngster was Ken Taylor, who used to play for Yorkshire. You never saw him diving about but his seemingly effortless style was certainly effective. His anticipation was brilliant and he moved to the ball so well that I rate him as highly as anyone I have seen.

Fielding can be hard work – especially in the one-day game – but there is no more demanding job in cricket than keeping wicket, simply because of the constant involvement. There is no place to hide and even if runs are not being scored, the man behind the stumps is likely to be concerned with every delivery bowled.

It is a specialist occupation and people are often guilty of forgetting this. The ball comes soaring in from the boundary or flies down the leg side and the wicket-keeper is expected to be in position, nonchalantly plucking it out of the air. No one bats an eyelid if he does this but as soon as the ball is fumbled, you can hear the groans. Although the top wicket-keepers make the job look easy, you only need to see someone less proficient operating behind the stumps to realise that this is far from true.

I discovered this the hard way when England were touring India and had three players injured in the same match. There was a vacancy for a wicket-keeper and I fancied the job, figuring that my agility would enable me to get by. It was only a matter of seconds before I had cause to regret my decision, however, because Mike Selvey sent the first delivery flying down the leg side. I felt confident of handling it but as I dived across to cut it off, the ball suddenly swung back after it had passed the stumps to leave me stranded.

The difference between taking the ball cleanly and fumbling it is incredibly slim, especially when you consider its size and the speed it is travelling. Yet the slightest error often means a cracked or bruised finger and that is an occupational hazard a wicket-keeper must learn to live with.

Wicket-keepers have to be hardy and they also need sharp reflexes, a reliable pair of hands and strong legs. They spend half their day crouching and the other half running back and forth from the stumps, so the strain on the leg muscles is obvious. Courage is another vital ingredient and this is often underrated. Not everyone can stand up to the spinners and concentrate on taking the ball when a bat is being swung in front of his face.

Derbyshire's Bob Taylor is a magnificent wicket-keeper, not only because he is remarkably competent at all times but because of the important part he plays in other ways.

Wicket-keepers are better placed than anyone to know how the pitch is playing and whether any particular type of delivery is troubling the batsman. This information can be invaluable for the captain and often influences the outcome of a match. Taylor is an expert at this and at keeping the fielders alert. He is quick to lead the applause when a throw drops over the stumps into his gloves but woe betide the man who makes him run or stretch.

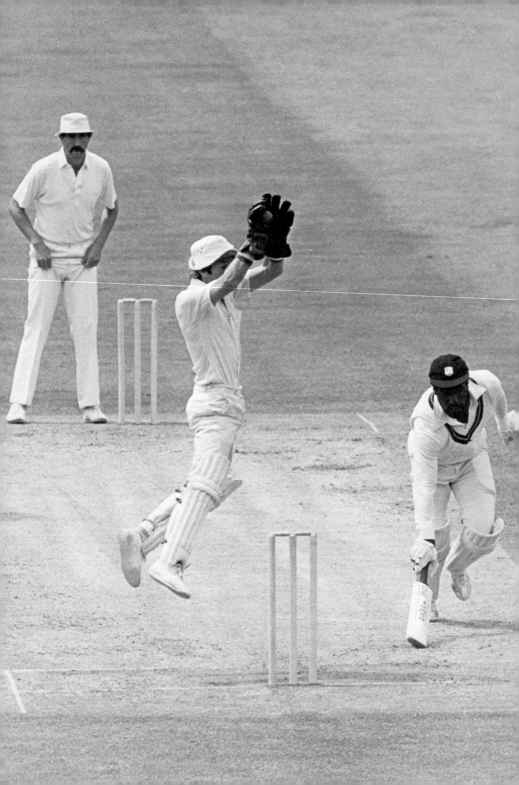

Such encouragement or reproof is vital, especially when the fielding side is having a difficult time. If a big stand is under way there is a natural tendency for despondency and slackness to creep into the fielding. But it is less likely to happen when there is a wicket-keeper like Taylor around.

Wicket-keepers, like everyone else in the field, have found far greater responsibilities thrust upon them since the introduction of regular one-day cricket. There is much more pressure on teams to prevent runs being scored and because of this, standards have improved immeasurably in recent years.

Fielding used almost to be regarded as a necessary chore by most cricketers and it is not that long ago that teams were prepared to carry 'passengers' providing they could bat or bowl effectively. The less talented fielder was simply banished to the outfield – out of harm's way – and if he could not stop the ball with his boot when it went in his direction, no one seemed particularly bothered.

In present day cricket, however, the man who cannot play a part in stopping runs being scored is rarely selected and virtually every county now demands a high standard of fitness from its players.

At Nottinghamshire, we introduced a schedule a few years ago and I would go so far as to suggest that any youngster who follows this with some degree of dedication and enthusiasm will become a better than average fielder. In fact, we adopted two schedules at Trent Bridge, the thirty minutes one which is used before the start of a day's play and the more concentrated sixty minutes one for use in practice sessions. Since these were introduced, every player on the staff has improved his fielding, if only because when the same situations crop up in a match, we have a better idea of how to handle them and react instinctively.

Bob Taylor shows his agility and safe handling as he gathers a high return. There is no more demanding job in cricket than wicket-keeping because of the constant involvement. The man behind the stumps is concerned with every delivery which is bowled by his team

Here is an outline of those schedules, together with other work which I recommend should be done throughout the year.

October–December

There is a natural tendency to eat more and spend more time sitting around during these three months so it is important to work at maintaining a reasonable level of fitness. I have been fortunate in recent years because I have been away on tour. But if I stay in England, I force myself to do enough basic training to keep me in reasonable condition.

Twice a week I do long-distance runs of about six miles and along with these are shuttle runs which require sprinting and turning. In this way, you can maintain stamina and sharpness at the same time. During this period it is also useful to devise a system of circuit training, whether you have the use of a gymnasium or lacking this, have to improvise.

January–March

This is the time to begin thinking about the new season and if you have been keeping yourself reasonably fit during the previous three months, you will see the benefit of it during this period of the year.

The weather is nothing like good enough to work outside, so try to get regular use of indoor facilities where net practice will enable you to work on your timing. At the same time, practise throwing at the stumps to get your arm functioning effectively again, placing the emphasis on quickness and accuracy.

Another priority at this stage of the year is to harden your hands. This is very important because in the cold April and May days at the start of the season, split fingers are a regular occurrence if the hands have not been properly prepared. It happened to me at the start of the 1979 season when, having just returned from the tour of Australia, I wrongly assumed my hands were in the right condition. I caught a ball awkwardly in our opening Benson and Hedges match against Middlesex, needed stitches in my hand, and did not play again for a few weeks.

52

Initially the only way to harden your hands is by tossing a cricket ball forcefully from one to another and if this is done regularly for a few days, your work in the indoor nets will finish the job.

April

County cricketers report back in April and our normal routine at Trent Bridge is to spend the first week at a nearby sports centre where we concentrate on getting fitness back to a peak.

During the second week we devote half of the time to stamina work, with a lot of running, and the remainder to sharpening up our fielding. This is when the sixty minutes schedule comes into daily operation and we have found that the best way to maintain interest and produce high standards is by devising fielding games.

May–September

The season is now under way and providing the right amount of work has been put in during the past seven months, we are ready to meet the demands of the next twenty or so weeks.

Even though we will be playing virtually every day during this period, there is no let up where fielding practice is concerned. Every match-day morning we will go through the abbreviated version and the sixty minutes schedule is followed on days off.

The thirty minutes schedule involves five exercises, the emphasis being at all times on quality.

No. 1 – This is a simple affair involving a line of players, properly spaced about 12ft from the batsman (striker), who keeps them busy with a succession of flat catches. It is important when fielding to keep your eyes on the ball and to concentrate. A good tip is to expect every ball to come to you.

No. 2 – This involves two rows of fielders who are fairly well spread out – two at the back and three in front – with the striker and wicket-keeper some 20 yards away. The idea is for the striker to clip the ball into the gaps, where it is caught or fielded and returned accurately to the wicket-keeper. We normally turn this into a game, seeing who can catch the most.

No. 3 – The five fielders are stationed together about 25 yards

Derek Randall demonstrates the style which has earned him so many run-out victims during his career. The fielder should always attack the ball rather than wait for it to come to him but while speed is important, the top priority is to ensure that the ball is correctly gathered. Only then should he take aim at the target and with a sharp, accurate throw, the batsman will always be in danger

from the striker and wicket-keeper and the ball is played along the ground into different areas. It involves sprinting to the ball, picking it up, and producing an accurate throw. This is a tough exercise because we do three of these, take a minute's rest before doing four more, and then five more after another brief rest.

I probably work harder at this than at any other exercise because it is the type of situation I often come up against in a match and it is important that I can do it to a high standard.

Two of the essentials are to attack the ball – not wait for it to come to you – and to make sure it is in your hands before you think about your next move. I often see youngsters who are so busy thinking about a run-out possibility that they take their eye off the ball and end up fumbling it. You cannot do a thing until the ball is in your hands – then is the time to look at your target.

Once the ground fielding aspect of this exercise is complete, the same positions are maintained to practise high catches. Again, it entails a sequence of say three-four-five with a short rest period between each, the only difference being that the striker will loft the ball and the fielder must be in position under it.

No. 4 – On this exercise, the striker gives the fielder a short-range catch rapidly followed by a long one in which you are either running backwards or trying to watch the ball over your shoulder.

Top priority in attempting a catch is to keep your eyes on the ball at all times. The catch should be taken as high as possible (in front of your face) and the fielder must then 'give' with the ball and bring it into his chest

An under-arm throw can be most effective, providing the distance to the wicket is not too great. This method enables the ball to be released more quickly and accurately. The majority of Derek Randall's run-outs have been achieved in this way

Overhead catching is exceptionally difficult and the rule is to keep your eye on the ball for as long as possible. This one-short-one-long sequence is also used for fielding and again, the quality of returns to the wicket-keeper is important.

No. 5 – Slip catching is the final exercise on the thirty minutes schedule, and this entails one man throwing the ball to the striker, who edges or hits it in the direction of the ring of fielders behind him. The thrower begins by throwing underarm to simulate a spin bowler and then switches to over-arm to get more speed.

A useful tip with slip fielding is that the wicket-keeper and first slip watch the ball all the way when a match is in progress whereas second, third and fourth slips watch the edge of the bat.

The sixty minutes schedule involves three additional exercises which are aimed primarily at improving the quality of the out-fielding.

No. 1 – This covers boundary fielding with the striker sending the ball a fair distance and the fielder being responsible for cutting it off and returning to the wicket-keeper. It is important to employ a second line of defence in this situation – especially on an uneven outfield – and to have the foot or body behind the ball.

No. 2 – Fielding practice can be fun at times and one of the most enjoyable exercises we engage in is: throwing at one stump. Someone rolls the ball out – ten to the right, ten left and ten straight – and it becomes a competition to see who gets the most direct hits out of thirty.

No. 3 – This is another exercise which invariably turns into a competition. The idea is to contrive a match situation with a bats-man attempting to score two runs and becoming involved in a race against the fielder.

The wicket-keeper rolls the ball out, judging things so that it becomes a good race, and the batsman must run two before the ball is returned and the bails dislodged. We normally pick two teams with everyone going twice. It can develop into a highly entertaining contest.

6

First-class Cricket

I would recommend the life of a professional cricketer to anyone, providing they have the necessary attributes. By this, I do not just mean an ability to play the game, because essential as this is, it is only one of many requirements.

As with most sports, there are plenty of people playing on the local parks who have the talent to play at the top level. But only a comparative few have the temperament and self-discipline to make a living from it. It sounds an attractive life – I happen to think there is none better – but not everyone can come to terms with waking up virtually every morning throughout the summer months, knowing that they have to go out and justify themselves.

The Schweppes County Championship is the bread and butter competition in which every team battles through twenty-two three-day matches in a season, to decide ultimately which is the most able all-round outfit in the country. Winning this requires every conceivable quality – character, resilience, determination and the ability to adapt to any conditions and still play positive cricket.

There is a lot less luck involved here than in the one-day game, and any team with weaknesses struggles to hide them. Three days can be a long time, and although this allows breathing space to recover from a difficult patch, no county wins the Championship without a good all-round blend.

Most players will tell you they get more enjoyment from the limited-overs variety of cricket, but we all know it is our first-class performances which keep us in a job. This is the arena where you show your full range of skills, and if you are ambitious in the sense of wanting to play Test cricket, this is where you are judged.

I get far more pleasure from playing Championship cricket these days, with the introduction of bonus points for batting and bowling and the decision to restrict the first innings of each side to one hundred overs. Previous to this, the odds tended to be so firmly stacked in favour of a draw that there often seemed little point in continuing with some games. Nowadays, however, there is nothing to be gained from playing for a draw and captains are making the type of declarations which lead to exciting finishes.

The whole business of three-day cricket is far more complex in every way as compared with limited-overs matches. Bowlers have to work for their wickets, as opposed to waiting for batsmen to give them away. But they have compensations. They can operate with the length of run which suits them best, and generally, they can afford to be more attack-minded because the cost of giving away a few runs is likely to be less severe.

At the same time, batsmen do not have to arrive at the crease with the feeling that they must crack the first ball to the boundary and attempt to hit the fastest fifty of all time. They can afford to be patient, play themselves in properly, and go about their work in a more thoughtful fashion.

From a personal point of view, I would love to see the crowds start flocking back to watch Championship games. It is always difficult when you arrive at an almost deserted ground, knowing you must make your own atmosphere. We are professionals and must play regardless of how many spectators are watching, but I must admit, I find this especially difficult after playing for England.

In a Test Match you are under pressure the whole time and the atmosphere is electrifying. Every move is seen and commented upon and the normal first-class game is so far removed from this that motivating yourself to produce your best takes a special effort.

The demands on players are much greater than they used to be. Counties in general are becoming more conscious of the need to be successful and although the rewards for this are increasing all the time, it is money which has to be earned the hard way.

Most professional cricketers are only employed for six months of the year and although the top men may earn enough to keep themselves going, the majority need to find alternative employment for the remainder of the time. Although this can be a problem I would suggest that the greatest occupational hazard is the pressure which is placed on a player's home life.

They tend to devote their lives to their job during the summer months and this entails a lot of sacrifices. Not only do we find we are often 'working' seven days a week but also, on most days when we are not actually playing, we are understandably required to turn up for training and practice.

Our normal working day for a home game starts at 9.30 a.m. when we must report to the ground and assuming a 6.30 p.m. finish, by the time we have changed and had a quick drink it is invariably eight o'clock before we arrive home. Moreover, a home fixture is often followed by an away one and that involves a rapid transfer to cars and a long drive to the hotel which will be our base for the next three days or so.

Even with better cars and motorways, travelling can be the worst part of the job. The players will probably not feel like driving anyway following a hard day's play, and after the inevitable late night, they are expected to be fresh and ready for action the next morning. Some clubs use coaches but at Nottinghamshire, we have a preference for cars. A coach does not normally travel as fast, and because the players tend to live over a wide area, we find it more convenient to use our own vehicles.

I am not complaining, for I have come to accept this as part of the job. If I tell you, however, that I have calculated that I spent just three months of 1979 sleeping in my own home, you will understand what I mean about the strain on a cricketer's family life.

I have the same sort of responsibilities as most men with a young son to bring up, and I am always conscious of the strain this puts on my wife Liz. She respects that it is my job and that it will not go on for ever. But my family are entitled to more of my time than it is sometimes possible to give them.

Because cricketers spend so much time together, a strong bond inevitably grows up between them. A sound team spirit is essential and although it would be unnatural if tensions did not creep in

(overleaf) Derek Randall hooks Lillee to the boundary during his innings of 174 in the Centenary Test at Melbourne in 1977

61

occasionally when things are going wrong on the field, they seldom last. The players are aiming at the same targets, and they share the frustrations and highlights. They become very close during the six months they are virtually living together, and it is a marvellous feeling when they combine to gain success.

A sense of humour is a very necessary ingredient in the make-up of any professional cricketer. No one escapes the dressing-room leg-pulling and you cannot afford to be sensitive when you are the target. Hardly a day goes by without someone bearing the brunt, and you come to accept it as part of the job. There was an occasion in the 1979 season, for example, when Nottinghamshire's fast-bowler Richard Hadlee was having a lot of trouble with a hamstring injury. He had not played for a few weeks and arrived in the dressing-room one day to find that someone had stuck a 'Butlin's' sign on his locker.

This is the type of thing which players have to put up with but it all helps team spirit. Although playing cricket is a serious business, it is important to be able to laugh and joke at the right time.

As individuals, we all go through a difficult spell at some stage and that is when we need the help and support of our colleagues. I remember a period when I went through four consecutive innings without scoring a run. My confidence was absolutely shattered and I was ready to give the game up.

It was stupid to think that way, of course, because this is all part of the game and you must have the determination to over-come such problems. Yet the experience of incidents like these teaches you to make the most of the good times. There will be so many occasions during your career when the whole world seems to be against you that it is vital to enjoy the successful moments when they come along.

This is the type of thing I mean when I speak of needing to have more than just ability if you want to be a professional cricketer. You need to have the temperament to handle such situations – and accept the disciplines which often make the job less glamorous than it might seem.

My normal routine on a match-day is to report to the ground with the other players at 9.30 a.m. and to go through a series of loosening exercises. At 10 a.m. I change out of my tracksuit and

64

head for the nets where the amount of work I do may vary. At the start of the season I will have about 15 minutes of hard practice with special emphasis on concentration and timing. In mid-season though, providing I am in reasonable form, I might just stay long enough to hit a few balls and get used to the light and pace of the ground.

In contrast, if I am struggling with my batting I will probably remain in the nets for up to half an hour. I may be unhappy about a specific shot and I will get someone to throw the ball to a spot where I can work on putting it right.

Once we have finished in the nets, the next job is to get all the players together and to go through our invaluable ritual of fielding practice which I mentioned in the previous chapter.

At 10.45 a.m., it is time to get ready for battle. We adjourn to the dressing room for a cup of tea and to change into clean flannels and shirt. Then the captain will issue his instructions and we are ready to go.

If we are batting and I am at No. 3, I follow a procedure which I find suits me best. In my early days I used to sit and watch every ball bowled until I realised that this was causing me to become too tense. Now I sit and watch the first few overs to check on the bowlers and conditions. It is important to know who is bowling and to get some idea about how the pitch is playing, but once that is done, I withdraw to the dressing room. It suits me to disappear into a corner with a newspaper, and although I am always aware of what is happening on the field, it helps me to relax.

Suddenly the big moment arrives. A wicket has fallen and I am the next man in. My pads are already in place so I put on my inner gloves, drop a cap on my head and snatch my bat and gloves. It is amazing how the adrenalin starts to flow at this time, no matter how experienced you are, and before you know it you are on your way down the pavilion steps.

What happens after the dreaded moment of dismissal depends on the state of the game. If we are chasing a target or fighting to avoid defeat I will sit and watch when I get back to the dressing room, whereas if nothing much is happening, I head straight for the showers.

I used to sit in the dressing room for long periods, trying to analyse why I had lost my wicket. This was something I had to learn to control, however, because there was a danger of it becoming an obsession. Although it is important never to stop thinking about how you can improve yourself, I feel you must try to find a happy medium.

We break twice during a day's play for lunch and tea. Eating can be a problem if you are not careful. Tea is not so bad because I just grab a sandwich and drink, though lunch can be difficult. After a hard morning's work in the field, I am normally ready for something to eat, but it is important not to overdo it. Salad is ideal, but at some grounds there may be a hot meal waiting for the players when they arrive in the dining room.

The medical experts say it takes about two hours to digest a full meal, so we have to discipline ourselves to refuse stodgy food. Apart from the obvious need to watch your weight, you cannot do yourself justice during the afternoon session if you have eaten too much.

Travelling is my pet hate, but without doubt the most frustrating thing about the life of a professional cricketer is that you are constantly in the hands of the weather. No matter what games you might organise to occupy your time in the dressing room, there is nothing more boring than sitting around for long periods waiting for the rain to stop or for the ground to dry out. Obviously this is especially galling if you have a chance of winning the match, and even when it is spread over three days, the loss of a few hours can make a significant difference to the outcome.

Waiting for the weather to change is one of the less enjoyable things about cricket – but there are not too many of them. Being a professional cricketer can be demanding but it is a marvellous way to earn a living. The game has been good to me and I certainly have no regrets about choosing it as a career.

7

One-day Cricket

The person who inspired the idea of playing one-day cricket on a regular basis at senior level should go down in the history books as one of the most important figures the game has known. There is no doubt in my mind that I would not be earning a respectable living from cricket today were it not for him – and nor would anyone else.

There were plenty of purists ready to criticise the limited-overs game and maybe they had good reason. When it comes to simple economics, however, there is no case to argue. The facts are that cricket was dying as a professional sport in the early 1960s. People no longer had the time or inclination to support the three-day Championship matches and virtually every county club in the country was in financial difficulty.

A situation of this kind soon snowballs and it was rapidly reaching the stage where the most promising young players were rejecting the opportunity of a place on the county staff because wages were slipping below subsistance level.

Suddenly, in 1963, the Gillette Cup appeared on the scene and this was the start of a remarkable transformation. The public responded immediately to this instant form of cricket and grounds throughout the country started to fill again. The attraction was understandable because not only did it offer the spectators a more urgent and exciting form of action, it also provided them with the opportunity to watch the game from start to finish, assuming the weather did not interfere.

Sussex soon got to grips with the revised version of the game and there was a boom in interest on the south coast as they carried off the trophy in the first two seasons.

Despite resistance in some quarters, it was inevitable that other competitions of a similar nature would follow and in 1969, the John Player League was introduced with the same immediate degree of success. The authorities were forced to accept that this was what the public wanted and with sponsors eagerly pouring money into the game, the facts could not be ignored.

Since then, of course, the fifty-five overs Benson and Hedges Cup was started in 1972 and two money-spinning and immensely exciting Prudential World Cup competitions have been staged in England.

The spectators loved the new style of instant cricket – and so did most of the players. It took some a while to make the transition from one variety to another and in the meantime, Jack Bond's Lancashire were collecting most of the honours. They scored a hat trick of Gillette triumphs and twice won the Player League in the space of four remarkable years, although it was not long before others began to adapt to the new way of doing things.

Kent, with their strong squad of talented players, have probably been the most successful county at the one-day game but as tactics began to play an increasingly more important part, it was not insignificant that Ray Illingworth should lead Leicestershire to four trophy successes.

The one-day events have now become accepted as major dates on the cricket calendar and a measure of their attraction is that the only two occasions on which Lord's is likely to be full to capacity during the course of a season are for the Gillette and the Benson and Hedges Cup Finals.

Counties have long since come to terms with the fact that they stage Championship matches for the benefit of hardened cricket followers and make their money from the eight Sunday fixtures, or if they are fortunate enough to get home ties, in the knockout competitions.

Instant cricket is here to stay and as one who was brought up in this environment and thrives on the atmosphere and excitement it generates, I am delighted.

As a professional player, however, I am acutely aware of the pitfalls and recognise that it is the responsibility of people like me to remind youngsters that this is not 'real' cricket. The game is all about striving to prove yourself better than the opposition over three or five days. The best team must win over this length of time but the same cannot always be said of the one-day variety.

Ray Illingworth, flanked by jubilant Leicestershire colleagues, parades the Benson and Hedges Cup. It was not insignificant that Leicestershire had considerable one-day success under Illingworth's leadership at a time when tactics were playing an increasingly important part

For this reason, I feel there is a danger that too much one-day cricket is being played at international level. Watching twenty-two of the world's finest players in combat in a limited-overs game is a magnificent sight but this must not be allowed to detract from Test cricket. It makes sense for, say, three abbreviated versions to take place during a tour, but it is vital that people keep things in perspective.

Because of the sudden upsurge in public interest, the one-day game has understandably taken on increasing importance. The rewards for success are high but from a player's point of view, it is important to try to maintain a balance between the two.

We are really talking about two separate games and few people find it easy to adjust from one to the other. A totally different approach and technique is needed for restricted overs games – mentally, as much as anything. When batting, the whole business revolves around taking risks and scoring as quickly as possible, while the bowlers' priorities change completely as they concentrate more on keeping down the run-rate than on trying to take wickets.

The forty-overs John Player League is a crash-bang-wallop affair which is over almost before you realise it. I find that the best policy in this competition is to go out and attack the bowling from the start because there is no time to play yourself in or attempt to 'see off' a particular bowler.

Because most people adopt this approach it inevitably leads to defensive play by the fielding side. Some of their fast bowlers are already at a disadvantage in not being allowed to use the run-up which suits them best, and they tend to concentrate on accuracy combined with field placing which will make scoring especially difficult. It is rare indeed to see a slip or any other close fielders employed in John Player League games, the sole aim being to restrict the scoring.

Teams have become more tactically aware over the years and while most use their best bowlers at the start and finish of an innings and have fairly standard field placings, it did not take them long to realise that much greater emphasis needed to be placed on aspects of play which were regarded as almost irrelevant in Championship games. For example, running between the wickets and fielding are now reckoned to be match-winning qualities. Scoring twenty quick singles or saving twenty runs in the field can make all the difference when the final scores are tallied.

One-day cricket is extremely demanding for the players. A lot more energy goes into your work for obvious reasons and you are constantly aware of the pressures. Whether batting or bowling, you cannot afford to waste a single ball and even just one mistake can prove costly for your team – especially on Sundays when there is seldom time to make amends for an error.

The Gillette and Benson and Hedges competitions are much more like a game of cricket in the true sense because they are played over a longer duration. You can afford to adjust your approach to some extent and have more scope to express your ability in a proper manner. With the bowlers able to operate from their full run-up, the new-ball carries far greater significance. The teams employ an attacking field from the start and if the need arises to switch to defence midway through the innings, then they will do so.

I am a supporter of one-day cricket and for sheer enjoyment, there is nothing to beat it. I would not pretend that it does not have its drawbacks, however, because it can – and does – lead to bad habits and therefore affects the chances of players making the grade where it really matters.

This is especially true in batting where, for example, it is not uncommon to see a player collect useful runs with an angled bat outside off stump on a Sunday afternoon, and then be dismissed, caught at slip, when playing exactly the same shot in the following day's Championship game.

Adjusting from one kind of cricket to another is no easy matter and it causes me some concern that the one-day game seems to have become the platform for launching a young prospect into senior cricket. Newcomers often notch up half a dozen Sunday games before they are looked upon as good enough to hold down a place in the first-class team and I maintain they are learning their cricket in the wrong surroundings.

They are thrust into the playing arena with a brief to score a rapid twenty or so and rush around the field. Similarly, a bowler is encouraged to bowl accurately rather than to attempt to take wickets, and while this is perfectly understandable, it can at the same time seriously impair his development.

This is particularly true in the case of a young batsman, who may be successful in what he sets out to do and will quickly earn a reputation with the spectators, the majority of whom only watch him in action on a Sunday. In the real sense, however, he has achieved very little and it is absolutely vital that he realises it.

Championship cricket calls for different priorities and proving your capabilities against bowlers flying in off their full run is a totally different proposition. A batsman must know how to graft for his runs and to show self-discipline and consistency if he wants to make it to the top, and I wonder if it is possible to learn these essential tricks of the trade in the one-day game.

71

Cricket is alive and well thanks to the introduction of the limited-overs competitions which, in turn, earned the support of the public and some wealthy sponsors. As a result, the players have been committed to playing virtually seven days a week throughout the summer months. But you will not hear us complaining because we realise we owe someone a vote of thanks.

8

Test Cricket

Every sports-minded schoolboy dreams of the day when he will represent his country and I was certainly no exception. I used to play those one-man Test Matches in my back garden and regularly produced a cultured century against Australia to win the Ashes for England.

It was all fantasy, of course, but once I joined the Nottinghamshire staff, my yearning took on a new dimension. I had crossed the vital hurdle and having broken into county cricket and established myself in the team, it meant I was within touching distance of achieving my ambition. I never stopped dreaming even when there was still some way to go, yet I realised at that stage that it was up to me whether I played for England.

Dedication and hard work were needed as never before but when I had a reasonable season in 1976, people suddenly began talking about me as a Test candidate. On reflection, I emerged with perfect timing because England had gone through a torrid experience against the West Indies' quick bowlers during the Tests that summer, and by the time it came to the end of season Prudential Cup matches, there was pressure on the selectors to introduce some younger players.

Of all the marvellous moments I have had in cricket, I doubt whether anything compares with the thrill of learning I was in the England squad for the first time.

It is difficult to describe accurately the feelings of elation and anticipation, mingled with apprehension, as I set off to Scarborough for the first of the one-day internationals. If, however, selection to the squad was my happiest moment, discovering that I was to be twelfth man probably ranks as my greatest disappointment.

This setback was only temporary however, and two days after

England had been convincingly beaten, I was on the score-card at No. 6 as we set out to avenge that defeat.

I managed to pick up a couple of catches as West Indies made 221 but this did not save me from a sudden attack of nerves as I marched out to bat. We were in desperate trouble at 31–4 at the time and to make matters worse, the light was appalling. Our position seemed so hopeless that perhaps it lifted some of the pressure from me, and after managing to survive until play was called off for the day, I stayed on to make 88 when the match resumed on the Sunday.

England lost again, as we did in the final Prudential game at Edgbaston, but after scoring 39 out of a total of 173 at Birmingham, I was honoured to be named England's Man of the Series.

According to many experts I had arrived. But I refused to accept that the selectors would include me in the party to tour India, Australia and Sri Lanka that winter until it became official. Deep down, I felt I had done enough to justify selection, but in this game you soon learn to take nothing for granted.

The fact that I had shown myself to be capable of knocking the ball around in a one-day game against widely spread fields did not necessarily indicate that I had the qualities required to play Test cricket.

I knew the selectors would give serious consideration to this as they made their choice for an arduous tour, and whereas my selection for the one-day games had been a thrill, I remember that being told that I was in the Test party came as a tremendous relief.

So I was actually going on tour with my country. All those schoolboy fantasies were about to be fulfilled, and although I still had to prove myself at the highest possible level, I was approaching what for any cricketer has to be the pinnacle of his career.

To be picked to play for England was the absolute ultimate as far as I was concerned, although I quickly learnt that there was no time to stand around admiring my achievement. I recall being

Every cricketer dreams of making a Test century but few have their wishes fulfilled. Derek Randall is pictured hooking against Australia on his way to scoring 150 during the 1978–79 tour. Randall's innings at Sydney inspired England to the victory which clinched the Ashes

75

instantly aware that I held one of eleven coveted positions. I was privileged and I knew it, yet at the same time I realised only too well that there were thousands of young hopefuls striving to step into my boots.

To a large extent, reaching the top in any sport is easier than staying there. This stands to reason since standards always improve. But until making that first overseas tour, I never fully appreciated what it takes to hold your own at Test level.

The game is in so many ways entirely different to county cricket and the most startling thing to a newcomer is the sheer quality of the play.

In a county match, a batsman normally has to worry about only two or three top-class bowlers who must be treated with special respect; against the others run-scoring will be easier. In Test Matches, however, the batsman deals continually with bowling of the highest quality, and the same applies to other aspects of the game.

The general fielding standards are exceptional. Catches are dropped comparatively seldom and a young batsman soon comes to accept that the stroke which scores four runs in a Championship game may not be good enough at international level. The sudden realisation of this can be frightening, and it is not unknown for capable cricketers to begin doubting their own ability when it becomes apparent that they are moving in totally different circles.

Similarly, bowlers discover that they are competing against batsmen who will not surrender their wickets in a moment of madness. The likes of Geoff Boycott are quite capable of occupying the crease all day without making an unforced error, so it takes something special on the part of the bowler to remove them.

In a five-day Test the batsman knows he can afford to be patient. The emphasis is on concentration and he has time to build an innings at the outset, knowing that the team who bat longest are generally successful. He can afford to defend and wait for the bad ball, yet these normally come so occasionally that it is essential for them to be dispatched to the boundary.

While the pressure on players to achieve things in a hurry is considerably less than in the domestic game, the overall strain involved in competing in a Test Match bears no comparison. From start to finish in a Test, the players are under enormous pressure. Apart from the huge crowds, every detail is covered extensively by the media and no one escapes for a second.

There have been players who found this non-stop pressure unbearable and I can understand this. My philosophy, however, is to concentrate on doing my best; and I find that if I am concentrating properly, the spectators just become part of the scenery. At the same time though, I am always aware of a very special atmosphere, and one of the most satisfying things about Test crowds is that they always seem to be so knowledgeable and appreciative.

The build-up to a Test in England normally follows a pattern. The team is announced about lunch time on the Sunday before the match is due to begin and for many of the players, a radio announcement may be their first confirmation of selection.

Those who are doubtful about their position normally get a phone call the night before, however, so that the news does not come as a complete surprise. If it is your first call-up to the squad, or if you have been dropped, the captain takes personal responsibility for letting you know in advance, and this is followed up a couple of days later by a letter from the chairman of selectors.

All necessary details about where you are staying and what time you must arrive etc, are contained in his letter. The normal procedure is to report to the venue for the Test on the Wednesday afternoon at 3 p.m. The touring side will have had their net practice in the morning, and England will move in after lunch for a session, which is as important for renewing acquaintances with team-mates as it is for sharpening up your fitness.

Certain formalities like posing for photographs and speaking to the Press must be dealt with and after getting changed and taking tea at the ground, the players adjourn to the hotel which will be their base for the next six days.

At 6.30 p.m. sharp there is a team meeting which tends to be a very lively and enlightening session, lasting anything up to forty-five minutes. The object is to discuss tactics for the forthcoming match, and nothing is left to chance. Each individual in the opposition line-up is talked about, along with anything else connected with the game, and all the England players have the opportunity to have their say.

The team meeting is followed by the traditional pre-Test dinner for the selectors and players, but we are on our way to bed by 10 p.m. I always ring home to check that my wife has no problems and then settle down for an early night, well aware of the demanding day which lies ahead.

Hopefully we manage a good night's sleep and after a sensible breakfast the following morning, we set off for the ground to arrive at about 9.30 a.m. By then the atmosphere will already be building up, and it serves as a sharp reminder that we are there to represent our country in a five-day event which will be monitored in all parts of the world.

We all go through our usual routine of fitness training, nets and fielding practice and then return to the pavilion to prepare for a day which, for every one of us, could have a major influence on our future career.

9

Touring

It usually raises a laugh when I stroll around Trent Bridge in November wishing everyone Happy Christmas. But there is a less amusing side to preparing for an England tour. Saying goodbye to your wife and family, knowing you will not see them for the next four months, is not the easiest of things to do.

You have to come to terms with it, however, because this is part of the job. Only sixteen or so players every year are privileged enough to be in this position and it is a marvellous feeling to know you are going abroad to represent your country.

Once the touring party is announced, it is not merely a matter of turning up a couple of months later to catch the plane. An immense amount of organising and arranging has to be done, not least to ensure the welfare of your family while you are away.

Because of the obvious demands on a cricketer's time during the summer months, many of the everyday jobs which need to be done at home tend to be neglected. The priority for me at the end of a season is to put this right and especially if I am going on tour, I try to spend as much time as possible with my family during the two intervening months.

My responsibilities to my family take preference over everything, but if I accept an England call, it is my duty to travel abroad determined to do my best. I cannot afford to spend the next four months worrying about whether everything is in order at home, so I must make arrangements in advance to ensure they will be covered in an emergency.

It is obviously important that I do not allow my fitness to lapse once the English season has finished and I make a point of going to Trent Bridge most days for a couple of hours training. There is also a long list of things which must be done and I have learned from experience that it is best to get each of them crossed off and avoid a last-minute rush.

Passports and visas must be in order, and each member of the touring party must undergo a stringent medical before leaving. It is necessary to have a series of injections and a complete dental check, because you do not want to be bothered by problems with your teeth when you should be concentrating on playing cricket.

Filling in forms seems to become a never-ending task for a few weeks – then comes the problem of packing. Because you are living in hotels and constantly transferring from one to another, it is important to take as little as possible.

Cricket equipment alone can be bulky with bats, pads and crash helmets plus a good supply of playing kit, and if you take too many everyday clothes, life becomes a seemingly endless round of packing and lugging baggage around. The secret is to take only that which will be essential during four months abroad, though that is much easier said than done.

Regardless of which part of the world you are bound for, the temperatures are likely to be considerably higher than during a typical English summer. The tendency in this case is to assume that less clothing than usual will be needed but even this is not necessarily true. Because of the extra humidity, a regular change of clothing is often required.

Once the packing is complete and arrangements have been made for the welfare of the family, you are almost ready for take-off. The normal procedure is to report to Lord's the day before leaving to finalise last minute details. This involves a briefing from the tour manager, who discusses the itinerary for the next four months and lays down the rules and regulations. Then the players sort out their equipment and after posing for the television and Press cameras, the England party are all set.

My first tour – to India, Sri Lanka and Australia – was the hardest but also the most enjoyable. I really had no idea what to expect and it was a tremendous adventure. Never for a moment did I forget that I was going abroad to represent England and perhaps that is the way it should be.

It takes two or three weeks to get properly acclimatised when you arrive at your destination, and although normally pressed into action within the first few days, you are only just about familiar with conditions by the time the First Test begins.

Perhaps the most memorable thing about touring is the marvellous feeling of companionship. No matter how hospitable the locals might be – invariably they are very friendly – the twenty or so who make up the England party remain isolated to a large extent. You are there attempting to show you are better cricketers than they are, and the Us v Them situation is always simmering in the background. Consequently the party becomes moulded into a very tight-knit group and it is difficult to describe the atmosphere accurately to someone who has never been a part of it.

For four months you live, eat and breathe with the other players and officials, and although you are obviously competing for places in the team, the feeling of togetherness is always apparent. It is standard procedure to swop room-mates regularly and, because of this, each player gets to know the others very well. It is important not to allow cliques to develop within the ranks but if two or three players come from the same county, this can easily happen.

Having the right atmosphere within the camp is vital, otherwise the tour can be an absolute disaster. There are enough people trying to plot your cricketing downfall without bringing additional problems on yourselves.

I have been extremely fortunate during my time on the Test scene to tour with a great bunch of people. We have a laugh and enjoy ourselves without ever forgetting that we are out there to represent England. We are always conscious of the fact that people at home are following our progress closely and that it is our duty not to let them down.

Obviously there are times when you feel homesick. Inevitably during a long, exhausting tour you go to your room at night and wish you were back with your wife and family, enjoying a normal home life. This is the biggest drawback. But you are unlikely to do many tours during a career as a professional cricketer and it is important to make the most of them. They offer an opportunity to see the world and it is an experience not to be wasted.

You are ambassadors for your country and must act as such – on and off the field. Bearing in mind that you are constantly on the move from one hotel to another, there is an endless succession of receptions to attend in each place. Although the more long-serving members of the party may sometimes be renewing acquaintances, the team generally are constantly being introduced to new faces. Pleasant though this necessary courtesy may often be, it is extremely demanding, especially after a hard day's play.

I remember one occasion in India when close of play was 6 p.m. and we had to be at a reception twenty miles away half an hour later. We did not even have time to get changed properly before dashing off, and although this was exceptional, you learn to accept this type of thing as part of touring.

You get the opportunity to go sight-seeing from time to time but few have much energy to devote to this. Playing is hard work in higher temperatures than you are accustomed to, and because of this, the rare days off are often spent lounging in your hotel rooms. It is necessary to keep out of the sun and to try to regain your strength, knowing that you must start another five days of high-pressure cricket the following day.

Some players cope better than others but the heat can be a problem. When we called in at Sri Lanka during my first England tour, for example, I found it unbearable. Just twenty-four hours after arriving we played a one-day game and although I have no idea what the temperature was, I have never experienced anything like it. The heat and humidity were such that at the end of play, everyone just collapsed in a heap in the middle of the dressing room. We were all utterly exhausted.

The sort of things normally taken for granted at home can be major problems while on tour. Food and laundry come near the top of the list – two essentials for professional cricketers.

Food is not generally a problem in places like Australia, New Zealand and South Africa, but in India and Pakistan, they lead a totally different way of life. We usually take a large consignment

Bernard Thomas lends a shoulder to assist with stretching exercises – one of many roles that England's physiotherapist fills during an overseas tour. Apart from dealing with everyday injuries, he advises the players on their diets and is a vital member of the 'team' during four months away from home

of corned beef with us when we are visiting these countries, but even so, Bernard Thomas, the England physiotherapist, is kept busy because we all suffer from bouts of dysentery at regular intervals.

Living out of a suitcase and never really having a chance to settle can make it difficult to keep a clean change of clothes. Apart from everyday clothes, it is by no means uncommon to change your shirt and flannels a couple of times during a day's play and they all have to be washed at some stage.

Equipment is important – players must look smart on the field at all times – but because you do not have an unlimited supply, incidents like one that occurred in India can be frustrating: flannels came back from the cleaners having shrunk a couple of feet, or with buttons missing, and although we had a good laugh about it, the people involved did not find it so funny.

These are the sort of irritations you constantly come up against while on tour and it is important not to let them distract your attention away from the most essential thing. You are there to play cricket on foreign territory in conditions to which you are unaccustomed. At no time is this easy because you are an international team with the spotlight on the players all the time.

To win a series while away on tour is a remarkable achievement and although people seemed only too willing to decry England's efforts in retaining The Ashes in Australia in 1978–79, I maintain that no victory overseas should be underrated.

10

Managers and Secretaries

It is more than coincidence that Kent, the first county to appoint a cricket manager, have won more honours than anyone during the past decade. They set an example which others have been forced to follow in order to compete on level terms.

They began by introducing a highly organised youth policy, which permitted no youngster of any consequence to slip through the net, and were rewarded when a steady stream of talented players emerged to establish themselves in the first-class team.

Success followed, inspired by the likes of Alan Knott, Derek Underwood and Bob Woolmer, and when this meant that Test calls 'robbed' Kent of several key players for much of the season, they soon found a way to overcome it. They accepted the inevitability of the situation, decided to employ a much larger than average playing staff, and managed to keep their finances in order by continuing to win trophies and pull in the crowds.

It sounds simple yet, at the time, they were revolutionary moves. They took a gamble but if anyone doubts their wisdom, you only have to look at how others have followed their example.

Every county has a youth policy now. Playing staffs seem to be increasing every year and it is only a matter of time before they all appoint a cricket manager.

Kent's long-term planning really began when Les Ames became manager. At first he combined his cricket duties with those of secretary but Colin Page later assumed control of playing affairs on a full-time basis.

The introduction of managers was long overdue and I am sure they will play an increasingly important part in the years ahead as the game rapidly becomes more professional and results more vital. Whether they will actually become as dominant as football

Les Ames was the first cricket manager and although combining the job with his duties as secretary, he sowed the seeds for Kent's immense success in the 1970s

managers remains to be seen. I feel that although the captain will always be the commanding figure on the field, there are all sorts of ways in which the manager will make his presence felt.

Having worked for the past couple of seasons with Ken Taylor as manager at Trent Bridge, I hope we never revert to the situation where the captain is in total control on and off the field. I do not say this for any reason other than the fact that the job is too big for one man.

Under the old system, the captain was responsible to the committee for all playing affairs. He looked after team administration, sorting out hotel arrangements, picking the team, working out the tactics and so on. At the same time, he was supposed to be producing a respectable personal level of performance on the field, and the burden on him must have been intolerable.

Vital little jobs did not get done because he was unable to devote time to them and the situation clearly called for a man, well educated in the affairs of cricket, to act as a buffer between players and committee.

A large proportion of the manager's job is administrative. He is responsible for handling cricket matters throughout the club, and this does not mean just the first team. Unlike the captain, he has time to devote to 2nd XI and Colts players and having set up a sound youth policy, will ensure that it continues to run properly.

His presence means that youngsters get a much better deal than they did a few years ago. To begin with, they have a greater chance of being discovered and having joined the staff, their progress will be monitored closely. The manager will see that they get the guidance which will enable them to develop their talents, and although it will put the young players under greater pressure to justify their place on the staff, this is how it should be.

Judging from personal experience, the advent of managers has resulted in far more organisation within cricket clubs, and the players appreciate this. It is inevitable, for example, that they will have personal problems from time to time and under the old regime there was no telling when or how they would be dealt with. The captain, already overburdened with his own worries, would need to refer things to the committee, and that could take anything up to a month. In comparison, five minutes with the manager now and

Colin Page (standing far right) with the Kent team. When Colin Page took over as full-time cricket manager of Kent, he followed through Les Ames' early ideas and set standards which other counties have followed

a problem is dealt with straight away, enabling the player to get on with the job which matters.

It is vital that the manager and captain have a sound working relationship because although the manager is in charge – and the security of his job will ultimately depend on results – he can only do so much about performances on the field.

He selects the playing staff and might even pick the team. He can ensure the players reach and maintain the correct level of fitness and dictates the standards of discipline off the field. Once the game begins, however, it stands to reason that the captain must assume complete control.

In most cases they liaise closely on team selection and tactics but the captain is the influential figure on the field. The result of a match will often hinge on how the captain decides to use his bowlers or set his field and the manager must leave him to solve those problems as they occur.

Just as the cricketing side of things has become considerably more professional in recent years, so the same can be said for the administration of clubs.

The opposite number to the cricket manager is the secretary, and his 'job definition' has altered drastically as the outlook of clubs becomes geared so much more towards raising money. No longer are they simply responsible for paying the wages, dealing with gate receipts and making sure that all relevant forms have been filled in.

Top priority these days is the establishment of a system which will bring in enough cash to keep the club in business, and this means dealing with sponsors and ensuring that an effective fund-raising scheme is in operation. At Nottinghamshire, for example, the income from these two sources is considerable, though also relevant in this respect are a squash club and bar, a souvenir shop and our own club newspaper. It requires a fairly large staff to administer these things yet they all contribute vital income to the club and make the secretary's job today incomparable with what it was even five years ago.

The administrative work also needs to be done, but that is only a part of the secretary's modern function. Inevitably, clubs are now employing people with considerable business expertise to do this job, and the financial performance of each county depends on how they cope.

11

Captains

Despite England's considerable success under the leadership of Mike Brearley, he has never been short of critics. There always seems to be someone trying to make out a case for having him removed and I have never been able to understand this.

Perhaps it stems from ignorance, for I can only imagine that those people really have little idea about what is involved in captaining a Test team.

I am not trying to make out that Brearley has an outstanding record as a Test player, although he is a far better batsman and slip fielder than many have been prepared to accept. Yet when you add his cricketing knowledge and outstanding leadership qualities to his useful batting contributions, there is no doubting his value to the team.

The captain is the key man in the team, regardless of the level of cricket being played, and when a country embarks on a major tour, this position assumes enormous importance. Touring is an incredibly tough business from the point of view of the number of matches played, the quality of the opposition and the fact that you are on your own in a foreign land.

The only way the team will survive and be successful is if the organisation is absolutely right, on and off the field. Playing tactics must be correct at all times and maintaining the team spirit throughout four exhausting months is essential. If things go wrong in any of these aspects it could have tragic consequences and the man with most control over the situation is the captain.

Brearley sees it as his priority to get the best out of individuals and blend them into a team. He has done this brilliantly over the years – often at the expense of himself. For example, my first two Test centuries were scored in Australia and it just happened that

Mike Brearley, constantly thinking of ways to outwit the opposition, adjusts the field from his slip position. An outstanding leader with a remarkable knowledge of the game, he has proved his ability to get the best out of individuals and blend them into a team

91

Brearley spent much of the time at the other end when I was making them. He was more bothered about me than himself, constantly advising and encouraging me, and if it had not been for his help, I might never have got those centuries.

No matter what the ability of individual players, a team very often has to stand or fall by the decisions the captain makes. Not only must he know the game backwards, he also has to understand what motivates each player and be able to use their strengths to the team's advantage. He is never far away from pressure and his ability as a captain can best be judged by how he reacts to this.

I cannot recall seeing Brearley under greater pressure than when England were in Australia for the 1978–79 tour. We had won the first two Tests without too much difficulty but they won the third and were well placed to square the series in Sydney.

We were all out for 152, Australia made 294 and the pressures built up to such a pitch that many people would have cracked. Outwardly though, Brearley never flinched and his mood of confidence got through to the other players. Geoff Boycott was out without a run on the board in our second innings, but I managed to share in a stand of 111 with the captain and we went on to clinch The Ashes.

Especially at times like this, the captain needs to be an inspiring figure.

The arrival of managers on the domestic scene has removed much of the unnecessary responsibility from captains, but whether it be in a Test, Championship or one-day game, they still have much to consider in addition to their own performances.

The players will arrive at the ground, change at their leisure and go through their fitness routines to be ready in time for the start of play. The captain, however, has numerous duties to attend to. Apart from any essential administrative work which must be carried out or delegated, he must select the team and decide whether it is best to bat or bowl if the toss is won.

Most counties normally have twelve players in readiness on the first day and make their final selection on the morning of the match. Once the captain has checked the weather forecast and assessed the conditions, he will make his choice of playing an extra spin bowler or seamer.

Perhaps he will be unsure about what to do if the toss is won, and although this means consulting with his senior players in advance, the final decision is his responsibility. Once this has been made, it is up to the players to give their complete backing to the captain and to carry out his instructions.

If the team is batting first, he may have cause to adjust the batting order to suit certain situations, but basically this is a comparatively relaxing period when he can concentrate on his own performance.

It is a different matter when the captain leads his team on to the field, however, because the events of the next few hours – or days – will be engineered by him. Bowling changes and field placings are his responsibility and he will be constantly thinking of ways to get the better of the opposition. To do this requires an expert knowledge of his own players and the ability to use this to best advantage. He must also have an awareness of the strengths and weaknesses of each opponent and be able to adjust his tactics accordingly.

This is one of the great attributes of Brearley and hardly a moment goes past on the field when he is not thinking about his options. Fielders must always keep an eye on him because he continually makes slight alterations which will have an unsettling affect on the batsman.

The responsibilities of a captain have increased enormously since the introduction of the one-day game. Things happen at such a rapid pace in a forty-overs match that it is often difficult to keep track of the constantly changing position – but the captain must, while anticipating what might happen next. There are very many alternatives to consider because events are nothing like as orthodox and predictable as in the three- or five-day game.

The bowlers are only allowed to bowl a set number of overs so that side of things must be properly organised. Meanwhile, field placings continually need to be changed. When batting, the required run-rate is always uppermost in your mind and a sudden change of approach might be needed to influence the way the game is going.

One wrong decision – especially on a Sunday – can make all the difference, and this is another illustration of the value of a good captain. If you have one who makes the correct decision nine times out of ten, then you are half-way to being successful.

93

A typical attacking stroke from Gary Sobers who, when captain of West Indies and Nottinghamshire, was the finest all-rounder in the world. He believed in leading by example and commanded respect by his outstanding ability

There are various types of captain and they tend to fall into two main categories. There is the thoughtful, knowledgeable type – like Brearley and former Leicestershire captain Ray Illingworth – who command things on the field in a cool, calculated manner. They set high standards and demand that others maintain them.

In contrast to this is the man who, though perhaps less tactically aware, will lead his team from the front. It takes a special person to do this and the best example I can think of is Gary Sobers, who was captain of Nottinghamshire when I joined the staff.

He was a great believer in natural ability, of which he had an abundance. If things were not going well, his answer to it was to stroll out and make a century or put himself on to bowl and take a couple of wickets. It inspired each member of the team to do everything in his power to ensure that Sobers's efforts were not wasted.

12

Umpires and Scorers

There are no more important figures in first-class cricket than the umpires and scorers. Quite simply, without them the game could not function.

I would say that without exception they are deeply in love with cricket. In most cases they are former players who have retired but wish to remain involved in the game.

They are in the background most of the time and perhaps this is how it should be for spectators pay to see the players perform. But never underestimate the value of umpires and scorers, nor the difficulty of the jobs they carry out to an exceptionally high standard.

They need powers of concentration at least on a par with the players and quite possibly, by the end of a week, they will have used up more mental energy. The players at least get a break at some stage during the game, whether they are batting or bowling, but there is no place to hide for the umpires and scorers. They are involved from the first to last ball every day, and their responsibilities do not only revolve around what happens on the field.

Normally, these often forgotten men of cricket are among the first to arrive at the ground. The umpires will check that everything is in order before play gets under way and on most occasions, they will have travelled a considerable distance to arrive at the venue by 10 a.m.

Once play starts, assuming conditions are suitable, they know they will be expected to spend the best part of the next eight hours giving unwavering attention to their job. That in itself is difficult – not everyone could do it – yet when you consider some umpires are moving towards retirement age and will be 'working' in extreme heat or cold on many occasions, they do a remarkable job.

I think the highest compliment I can pay them is to say that throughout my career, never once have I been able to catch them out. Never once have I seen a ball bowled, looked towards the umpire, and felt that he was not concentrating.

Although all countries have good umpires, the English standard throughout the first-class game is without doubt the best in the world. They make mistakes like everyone else, but not too often.

Theirs is a job which I feel gets more difficult every year and although, hopefully, they will never quite become the equivalent of a football referee, there are times when the extra pressures in the modern game seem to be pushing them in that direction.

Umpires must count the number of deliveries per over, signal to the scorers, check for no-balls and so on. They have countless jobs to carry out during the course of a day but their main function is to decide whether a batsman is out once the fielders start appealing. This might mean being in position to give a ruling on a run-out but more often it involves an appeal for a catch or a leg-before-wicket decision.

As the bowler arrives at the crease the umpire looks down to check that the bowler does not overstep the mark. He must then adjust his sights to pick up the line of delivery and as an appeal goes up a split second later, give a snap decision. If I tell you that on numerous occasions players standing at slip or short leg have no idea whether the batsman has made contact with the ball, it provides a clear insight into the enormity of the task confronting the umpire.

There was a time when umpires were relieved of some of their responsibility because players tended to 'walk' immediately if they knew they were out. In theory it is the correct sporting thing to do and many still abide by this unwritten law.

There are two schools of thought on this, however, and it is not for me to say which is right or wrong. If an umpire is unsure it is his duty to say 'not out' and it seems to have become the done thing in certain quarters to stand and wait for a decision. The umpire is there to make that decision and in a sport where there is now much to be gained or lost from the eventual result, his verdict is all-important.

I must say, though, that I learned from experience that standing one's ground can often work against you. I made the mistake a few years ago of standing my ground when I knew I had got a slight edge, and although I benefited at the time, I am sure I suffered for that action in the long-run. Players get themselves reputations for this sort of thing and when umpires discover they are being 'conned' – and they usually do – they will not tolerate it. The next time you are involved in a fifty-fifty decision, they may not give you the benefit of the doubt.

Most umpires have played the game at the top level themselves and they know what is at stake for us. Although things get said and done in the heat of the moment, I always get the feeling that they know there is no malice intended.

I was involved in a nasty incident with Dusty Rhodes while playing for Nottinghamshire at Trent Bridge. It was in a Championship match against Leicestershire and they were a county against whom, at that time, I had never managed to score runs. I was determined to put it right that day and had worked hard to make twenty odd when I went to cut a ball, hit the ground, and got nowhere near it. The wicket-keeper and slip appealed for a catch and I had a few words to say to Dusty when he gave me out.

Even though I knew he was wrong, I went and apologised to him later because what I had done was totally inexcusable. He accepted my apology and deep down, I realised there was no way he would have intentionally given me out if he had not thought I had made contact with the ball.

Fortunately incidents of this kind are scarce in first-class cricket and the relationship between players and umpires is generally excellent. As former players, they have our utmost respect and most are not slow to offer advice at appropriate times. We mix socially and there is a bond of friendship, although everyone is well aware that a dividing line has to be drawn somewhere.

You can guarantee that when they get on to the field they will be totally impartial. They are professionals and carry out their duties to a very high standard.

They still retain a sense of humour though, and perhaps this is just as well remembering the occasion I hit Dickie Bird on the backside with the ball. I swooped to pick the ball up at cover, and as he moved smartly to get into position in case of a run-out, I did not notice him in my line of fire. It was on its way before I realised and poor Dickie was hopping around for at least ten minutes!

The umpires look so smart as they stroll out in their white coats and shoes but invariably they soon become weighed down by a collection of sweaters and caps. Their pockets are normally full of interesting items, including a light-meter which is the latest 'invention' for trying to combat one of cricket's most frustrating problems.

Umpires are not always the most popular people when spectators pay to get into the ground only to find that play has been held up because of a wet out-field or poor light. Until quite recently, it was left to their discretion to decide whether play was possible. In the case of bad light, meters now solve the problem for them.

From a personal point of view, I do not have tremendous faith in meters because although they provide an accurate reading in the near vicinity, the background is what really matters. The light may be reasonable in the middle of the wicket, but the batsman may still have to pick the ball up from a dark cloud behind the bowler's arm.

The importance of scorers, like umpires, is easily too under-valued. The game would quickly become chaotic if they did not carry out their duties to a high level of efficiency.

It takes a special type of person to do the job, generally an older man who is devoted to cricket. Concentration is vital, and he also needs to be conscientious and meticulous.

There is more involved in being a scorer than simply keeping a ball-by-ball check on the proceedings – although that can be demanding enough over an eight-hour period. It is also the scorer's responsibility to keep accurate up-to-date records, together with the averages of individual players which will be required by TCCB and certain journals.

The scorer must make himself available for answering regular queries from members of the Press and for numerous other jobs, like ensuring that the scoreboard is displaying the correct information. It can be difficult to keep up at times – especially during one-day matches – but he must always be in command of the situation.

Dickie Bird looks pleased to signal a dismissal during the 1979 Prudential
World Cup match between Pakistan and Australia. Umpires of his calibre
are vital to the success of cricket and the demands of the job should never
be underestimated

I remember discovering the hard way how demanding the job can be when I was detailed to look after the scoring in my younger days in club cricket. I became so engrossed in watching the game that I forgot to fill in some relevant figures and I was soon removed and replaced by someone more suitable.

There is a basic technique for scoring, but most devise their own system, which varies in the amount of detail shown. The Nottinghamshire scorer, Bill Thornley, travels around the country with us and is accepted as one of the lads and even plays a small part in tactics on occasions.

If one of us is working at a particular aspect of our game and wants a study done on how and where the runs are coming, Bill will draw us a map as the game goes along. This can also be applied to the opposition and if he is able to tell us, for example, that Fred Bloggs scores predominantly on the leg side between square leg and mid-on, we know that that area needs to be heavily patrolled.

There is more, much more, to scoring than simply acknowledging the signals of the umpires. Little things like keeping check on the over rates – teams are fined if they do not bowl enough overs per hour – and as I said earlier, cricket would soon become chaotic if the wrong men got hold of the pencil cases.

13

Equipment

The distressing sight of Indian all-rounder Mohinder Amarnath being stretchered off at Trent Bridge in an unconscious state finally convinced me of the value of wearing crash helmets.

The ball from Richard Hadlee which struck him on the head was only fractionally short of a good length, and it proved that against people of this pace, the slightest error of judgement can result in the batsman being hit.

Dennis Lillee struck me a glancing blow in the Melbourne Centenary Test, and I have never been able to forget the day when Colin Croft scored a direct hit when I was batting for Nottinghamshire against Lancashire in a Championship match at Old Trafford. I have often suffered recurrences of the type of headache and dizziness I felt on that day but even so, it was not until the incident at Trent Bridge that I was convinced I must pack a crash helmet when England embarked on the 1979–80 tour of Australia.

It was not that long ago when people laughed as Mike Brearley first appeared in a helmet, yet he ignored their jibes and maintained his belief in its value. Since then, helmets have rapidly become accepted as an important part of a cricketer's every-day equipment and there are numerous stories of players avoiding serious injury by wearing one.

For example, my Nottinghamshire colleague Trevor Tunnicliffe was involved in an incident a few years ago when he was fielding close to the wicket. The ball was driven in his direction and rebounded from the visor at the front of the helmet. Similarly, when Bob Taylor was hit on the head while batting for England against India at Lord's, it had absolutely no effect on him. But this sort of experience is enough to win anyone over. My reluctance to use one had certainly not been because I am braver than the average player, it was simply that when I tried them out in practice, I always felt inhibited, which has to be a bad thing for a batsman.

Apart from the problem of feeling uncomfortable, I was conscious of the way it shut out the noise and greatly restricted my vision. The fact that you are forced to look straight down the pitch when receiving is by no means a disadvantage, but I was bothered about other things. Because the ears are covered, I found it was not always easy to pick up my partner's call, and as the non-striker, the inability to glance around the field without deliberately turning my head was off-putting.

Mike Brearley was one of the earliest advocates of crash helmets and here he proves their value. The England captain was felled by this ball from Ghavri during the 1979 Test against India at Lord's but without protection, the injury would have been far worse

It took me a long time to decide that it was right for me to wear a helmet and I finally settled for the cap with ear-pieces, influenced by the knowledge that Australian wickets are quick and bouncy and England would be confronted by a variety of hostile fast-bowlers.

The moral of this story – as with so many aspects of cricket – is that you should do what suits you best, and provided you are satisfied of the need for crash helmets and feel comfortable wearing one, I would advise you to do so.

I cannot stress firmly enough the need to have the right equipment and to treat it with love and care. It so often follows that those who go to a lot of trouble over their equipment – including shirts, flannels etc. – will go to a lot of trouble over their game. If you feel neat and tidy in appearance, your game generally reflects the same pride, and I always feel that those who take the field with scruffy equipment are not really taking their cricket seriously.

I get through a fair quantity of playing kit during the course of a week and if my wife has a massive pile of washing by Monday morning, it usually means I am in good form. During a long innings I will invariably change my shirt, flannels and socks, and even my boots on occasions. They get warm and uncomfortable if you are in the middle for any considerable length of time and I reckon it is important that you should feel your best.

A cricket bat is the tool of my trade and I go to great lengths to make sure it is in the best possible condition. In fact, I normally have four on the go at any one time – all in various states of readiness.

Apart from the bat I am using, I will have one which is properly knocked in and ready to take into action in an emergency. Then I will have one which is nearly knocked in, and another that is almost new. I can then get them ready in the nets or in practice matches for when I need them. It is important that your bat does not get too dry in the hot sunshine and I usually give bats a coat of oil before I begin to knock them in.

Selecting a bat in the first place is something not to be taken lightly, and is certainly not a matter of picking up the first one which comes to hand. I think there is nothing worse than seeing a youngster using a bat which does not suit him. It needs to be the correct weight so that you can pick it up easily and swing it freely, and also you must ensure when selecting a bat that the rubber on the handle is firm so that it will not slip in your grasp.

There are various types of batting protection and as with bats, I often find that a youngster picks up the first piece of equipment available, or, in some cases, just does not bother. For example, a lot of boys go out to bat without wearing a box and that is the worst thing you can possibly do. It needs to be a solid metal box with cushioning around the outside.

The thigh pad is another item which is often disregarded and although it is a matter of personal preference whether you use it or not, it is asking for pain and trouble to under-value its importance.

It must provide adequate protection and needs to cover the whole thigh area to do the job properly. I have my own version of a thigh pad, by which I mean I ask my wife to sew an extra piece on the bottom, having suffered a few painful blows behind my left knee.

Similarly, I also make a slight alteration to my batting gloves to suit my preference. On most occasions I have been struck on the hand, the same two fingers have been unlucky, and they are now permanently swollen. Because of this, I insert some extra padding to save them from further damage.

When batting, I choose to wear inner gloves, which are similar to a wicket-keeper's except that they are fractionally thinner. I find they absorb the sweat, and bearing in mind the importance of keeping a firm grip on the bat, this stops the gloves slipping in my hand.

Pads need to feel comfortable and must not be so bulky that they restrict your freedom. They are understandably stiff when new, so I work on them for a while before I consider using them in a match. I manipulate them to begin with, which removes some of the stiffness, and fasten them tight and leave them for a period of time so that they bend into shape. I then wear them a few times in the nets to get them properly bedded-in and finally, once I am sure of the fit, I cut off any superfluous lengths of strap. It is important that there are no loose ends hanging around otherwise the ball might flick them, and cause you to be given out caught at the wicket.

14

Crowds

For me, there is no place like home and if offered the chance to play at any Test venue in the world, I would always come back to Trent Bridge. Nottinghamshire bias clouds my judgement, of course, but apart from happening to think it is a splendid setting for a big occasion, there is no greater thrill than playing for your country in front of your home crowd.

When England won the epic clash against Australia at Trent Bridge in 1977 it was the most magnificent day of my life. I managed to make the winning hit and that just about capped everything. Memories like that are not easily forgotten and although there are added problems involved in playing on your local ground, it all adds to the pleasure.

The pre-match pressures are greater because the local lad automatically becomes the centre of attention. He is the main target for interviews because it offers the Press a natural story. Also the number of people wanting to wish you well is seemingly endless. It all adds to the already intense pressures, because when the game is in progress you are constantly aware that your friends and relations are watching. They are anxious for you to be successful, and you are even more desperate not to let them down.

In the match I referred to against Australia, Geoff Boycott ran me out after I had made a good start to my innings on the first day. I was upset, of course, and felt desperately sorry for Geoff because it could have happened to anyone. At the same time

(overleaf) Spectators invade the Lord's pitch after the 1979 Prudential World Cup Final. The excitement of the one-day game has brought the crowds flocking back to our cricket grounds and they must not be allowed to drift away again

it removed some of the pressures from me because I knew that everyone realised it was not my fault. That was an irresponsible attitude which I now realise showed my inexperience.

Despite the extra problems involved in playing at home, I will never change my opinion. In fact, once I had achieved my life-time ambition of playing for England, my next major target on a personal level was never in doubt. I just dreamed of the day when I would score a Test century at Trent Bridge, knowing that if I achieved that before I ended my career, I would die a contented man.

Lord's is the accepted home of cricket and there is always something special about playing there, whether it be on a major occasion or against Middlesex in a Championship game. The place is so steeped in tradition that you cannot help but feel slightly overawed by it all. The atmosphere there when we played West Indies in the 1979 World Cup Final provided another memory which I will treasure.

After Trent Bridge, the English ground where I enjoy playing most, however, is Old Trafford. I always seem to do well there and find the Manchester people very friendly. They have a great sense of humour and appreciate it when the players respond to this in some way.

I have always regarded it as important that we relate to the crowd during the game. We are out there to do a job and this must obviously take priority, yet there is a time and place for everything and I feel there should be room for a touch of humour in cricket.

The attitude of English crowds has changed considerably over recent years and from a personal point of view, I reckon this is a good thing. It was inevitable that this would happen once the one-day game became established, and there now tend to be two different types of spectator watching cricket.

On the one hand you have the members, the three thousand or so who pay a subscription fee to their local county club at the start of a season, and are entitled to automatic entry to the ground and to certain other benefits at every home match. They are the staunch supporters who love the game and generally have time to sit and watch it. They appreciate the technical side of cricket and get great enjoyment from seeing a Championship game develop over the course of three days.

Members are a vital part of any club but in the past decade, other people have been attracted to cricket by the excitement of the one-day game and the likelihood of seeing a match decided on the day. They are a different breed and while many members tend to be somewhat staid and reserved in the traditional English manner, one-day cricket followers have the opposite approach.

They let their enthusiasm be known and because of the very nature of the limited-overs game, it is much easier for them to become involved and feel part of the proceedings. As professionals, we all enjoy playing in front of big crowds and I am sure it is true to say that we respond to the atmosphere which is generated. It becomes more like a football match at times, and although there has been criticism of this in some quarters, I am in favour of it, provided people behave sensibly.

Spectators in different parts of the world adopt differing approaches to watching cricket and whereas English crowds in general sometimes have difficulty expressing their emotions, the same cannot be said of West Indies supporters. They are fanatical about their cricket. They expect to see it played in a positive, adventurous manner, although they can often gain interest from the most mundane incidents. They like you to know they are there and while the noise can sometimes be off-putting, there is certainly no lack of atmosphere when West Indies supporters are around.

You find a similar crowd reaction in Pakistan and India, and I think it is easier as players to create a relationship with their spectators than anywhere in the world. They respond to the slightest sign of humour and their enthusiasm is infectious. They have had their problems with riots from time to time but are basically very patient people. It is necessary for them to be this way where cricket is concerned because batsmen normally dominate on the flat pitches in that part of the world, which means that the odds on a Test being drawn are always high.

Whereas players may set out to please spectators in India and Pakistan with friendly gestures, you soon realise that this is not the done thing in Australia. They are hard, forthright people, and you cannot afford to be too sensitive when you are playing in front of them.

I was warned of what to expect before my first trip to Australia,

109

but I still found out the hard way. We were playing a match in Perth, and Tony Greig sent me down to third man where I misfielded the ball the first time it came in my direction. I have never been subjected to so much abuse at any time in my life – I got the impression that they did not rate me too highly as a fielder! I was embarrassed to put it mildly, but there was a totally different reaction when the ball next came my way and I picked it up neatly and produced an accurate throw.

Perhaps it is because I have played many of my best innings in Australia that I seem to have a good relationship with the people. Their national characteristics come through in the way they approach their cricket and although they are uncompromising in everything they do, they are certainly appreciative when something is done to a high standard on the field.

For example, you can always tell when you arrive at an Australian ground during a Test Match which player has done well the previous day. They have a habit of sticking posters in every available place which makes some reference to the player's exploits and, in their own way, it is their tribute to his achievement.

Since the era of World Series Cricket, much more emphasis has been placed on keeping spectators happy – especially in Australia – and I feel strongly that this is the way it should be.

As players, we have a duty to entertain and provide value for money, and this approach must also extend to off-the-field activities. For example, I reckon that membership fees are far too low, but before considering increasing them to a realistic price, clubs need to take a hard look at the facilities they are offering in return.

Thankfully, the trend of spectators deserting the game seems to have been reversed. However, it is important that the authorities do not allow cricket to get into the sad state it was in during the early 1960s. Now that public interest has been revived and our grounds are starting to fill again, it is vital that every effort is made to keep the turnstiles clicking regularly.

Index

111